EARN YOUR MI|

Tom Raworth was born in Lo.
World War and has done everyt   ₉ ₛₗₙₑₑ. For half-a-
century he has printed, published, translated and written
poetry; has occasionally taught in several countries; and has
read his own work and performed with other artists all over
the world. He has a taste for spicy food from his father's
service in Burma and a quick temper from his Irish mother.
He is at the moment of no fixed abode. Last year, in Modena,
he was awarded the Antonio Delfini Prize for "lifetime career
achievement" though he is not yet dead.

Also by Tom Raworth

TOM RAWORTH
EARN YOUR MILK
COLLECTED PROSE

CAMBRIDGE

PUBLISHED BY SALT PUBLISHING
14a High Street, Fulbourn, Cambridge CB21 5DH United Kingdom

© Tom Raworth, 2009

The right of Tom Raworth to be identified as the
author of this work has been asserted by him in accordance
with Section 77 of the Copyright, Designs and Patents Act 1988.

This book is in copyright. Subject to statutory exception
and to provisions of relevant collective licensing agreements,
no reproduction of any part may take place without the written
permission of Salt Publishing.

First published 2009

Printed and bound in the United Kingdom by Biddles Ltd, King's Lynn, Norfolk

Typeset in Swift 10 / 12

*This book is sold subject to the conditions that it shall not,
by way of trade or otherwise, be lent, re-sold, hired out,
or otherwise circulated without the publisher's prior consent
in any form of binding or cover other than that in which
it is published and without a similar condition including this
condition being imposed on the subsequent purchaser.*

ISBN 978 1 84471 508 4 paperback

Salt Publishing Ltd gratefully acknowledges
the financial assistance of Arts Council England

1 3 5 7 9 8 6 4 2

for my grandchildren: Cato, Matilda,
Florence and Edward

CONTENTS

ACKNOWLEDGEMENTS

Parts of this book were previously published as

A Serial Biography
Fulcrum Press, London 1969 (Stuart and Deirdre Montgomery). Turtle Island, Berkeley USA 1977 (Robert Callahan)

Letters from Yaddo
O Books, Oakland USA 1987 in *Visible Shivers* (Leslie Scalapino)

The Vein
Translated by Catherine Weinzaepflen, published as *Le Filon*, CIPM/Spectres Familiers, France 1991 (Emmanuel Ponsart). The poem *The Vein* published by The Figures, USA 1992 (Geoffrey Young)

A Letter to Martin Stannard
Joe Soap's Canoe 14, London 1991 (Martin Stannard). *Removed for Further Study*, The Gig, Canada 2003 (Nate Dorward).

My gratitude to those publishers and further thanks to Miles Champion, master of the martini and the quesadilla, for doing what I would probably never have done; to Catherine Weinzaepflen and Emmanuel Ponsart for unearthing the faded only xerox of the English original; and to Matías Serra Bradford who kept things alive in Buenos Aires.

.

"Earn your milk."
— EDMOND O'BRIEN, *The Web*

A SERIAL BIOGRAPHY

'What I did there by way of writing, such skill as I had therein being placed at thy service—though yet, at times, it savoured still of the school of pride, as if panting after a round—my books bear witness; both those disputations, which I had with them that were present with me, and such as I composed by myself alone . . . '

— Saint Augustine

'And in English he announced he was going up shit's creek, with no engine, no sail, no boat and would they all wave goodbye.'

—J.P. Donleavy

'Then the whole world will belong to the people. Monsters of all kinds shall be destroyed.'

— Mao Tse-Tung

There are degrees of darkness, that's sure. Unreasonable. Think about it. The small room is inside the large one, and it is the large one that's—lightproofed?—that must be the word. So why is it darker . . . no . . . keep clear . . . why does it *seem* darker inside the small bed chamber? And not only that, but darker still when I shut the door? Dark and silence. I wonder if they checked the diet. Wind would be a bad thing. From their point of view, not mine. Brighten up the senses to wallow in a good fart. But it would break the silence unless ... no ... even they don't know that much. Jar the nostrils awake. And help the memory.

But it's easy enough. At first, after a few hours, I thought I might have gone blind. And how could I check? As I say, it's easy enough to get out. Ring the bell. They'll come. But then that's the end. The experiment is cancelled. In this darkness how can you tell if you still see? Answer: press your fingers on your closed eyelids. The coloured patterns are still there. Or can the blind do that? Still there ...

I got lost in there for a while. Watching them. Going deeper and deeper into the crystals. Your story they said. Now did they *tell* me that, or *ask* me, or just *suggest*? That's important to remember. And how will I keep track of time? By the number of meals I eat; the supply of food? But how often is it brought? Always when I'm asleep. It's never hot, so I can't go by that. Always a sandwich, a cold drink. And they leave it until I've finished. So if I slept through one complete day the same food would be there. Not even the bread goes stale in that plastic bag. And how long *do* I sleep? How can I *gauge* and *count*? Even outside, some nights I wake at 2 a.m. refreshed and force myself back to sleep for another five hours. Other times go right through the alarm. I don't want to smoke. It's forbidden of course. The glow would ruin the experiment. Though they could run a plastic tube in from outside. Like a hookah. Problems of soundproofing again. Unless on the other side of the wall they built another lightproof soundproof room. But what about the glow of the cigarette in *that* room if I looked down the tube? A right-angle bend in it? Or the smoke in cylinders? A system of valves open only when I suck? Anyway, like I said, I don't want to smoke. I wasn't surprised. Half (now why do I say half when I really thought all?) the pleasure is in seeing the smoke. I tried that years ago, smoking with my eyes shut. Not much enjoyment. So I wasn't surprised. But then I thought well, blind people smoke and seem to get something. Perhaps I *was* blind and if I had a cigarette I'd enjoy it and that would be the proof. But I got rid of that with a little pressure on the eyelids, like this . . .

Orange . . . Dark Red . . . Green . . . That's the complementary colour business I suppose. There must be something in there if I could just *focus* . . .

We are not supposed to talk aloud, or sing. Trust. Like those newspaper stands with coin slots. Why did I say *we*? *I* am not allowed to sing. Or rather, requested not to. Do they watch us, no, me? With infra-red or whatever they have. They're advanced enough in those ways. Must be something. Or how do they know when to bring in the food? Knock me out with odourless gas? No. If they could do that they could pump in cigarette smoke. They don't want me to be *too* uncomfortable. Yes they have the machines but they still have to put me in here on *trust*. On trust! That's what the man over the road used to say to his dog. Die for your country! And over on his back he'd go. A wire-haired terrier. Theirs was the only detached house in the street. His wife was Belgian and grew grapes in a glass conservatory in the garden. Middle-aged. Chic black dresses. I liked her. When television began again after the war she had me over every Saturday to watch. Nine inch screen. *Café Continental*. We want MUffin, MUffin the MULE. Dim in the room. Always a smell of curtains, carpets and deep old chairs. *Caesar* was the dog's name, I just remembered. Not Tray. That's what I thought it *should* be. And wherever I went, went my po-or dog Tray. My mother used to sing that. I nearly had a dog once. During the war. Arthur brought it for me one Sunday, he always came on Sundays. White with black patches. But I couldn't keep it. The bombs. The food. Played with it on the grass while he talked to my mother by the kitchen window. An old piece of tree trunk to hold the door open in summer. Behind the shelter a clump of gooseberry bushes. I hid with it there. But he took it back. I had a book once about a dog called Ginger. Another called Six Little Travellers. A white rubber doll called Bobby.

So how long do I sleep? Construct a clock. With what? Pulse rate is about 72 a second. Respiration 21 or 22. Breathing's the easiest. Can't hold my wrist all the time. Why not? Nothing else to do. I could hold my right wrist and still pick up the food. Though I once was left-handed. Still am for some things. Bow and arrow for instance. But the cold I had this morning has gone.

[4]

They were taking up the paving stones along the street. The skin is so thin; the earth and trees so powerful. With one heave the houses could all come down. So easy to wear a groove in the brain; the same relays click each time. For six weeks now there's been a poster on a wall near my home. In large black letters it says SUMMER ENTERTAINMENTS IN PARKS, and each time I read it as SUMMER ENTERTAINMENTS IN PARIS. Same thing with Shopfitters which I always read as Shoplifters. When I sense I'm going to bump into someone on the pavement the only solution is to look away and keep walking in a straight line. Once the eyes hold, all those dance steps and the final collision are inevitable.

August '66. Staring with my eyes out of focus (in this dark do I focus on anything?) through the train window. Raindrops trickling down look like floating puffballs. As we pick up speed their tracks swing towards the horizontal. Each back garden has thrown out a brick wall towards the train and captured a tree. Dank embankments, the earth dark. Looking back as the track curves, a narrow bridge vanishes into the foliage on either side, slightly out of true. Entering the tunnel. A grease smear on the window. My reflection blurred.

The way it *could* have gone, thinking like that. But no way left for the audience. What I want is a kaleidoscope, not a telescope. Now, their tracks merging with the gloom, the drops move across the glass like ball-bearings over black oil. Not right for this time.

What I must do. Is. Investigate the shape of a life. Somehow reach the solid body. Like the machine they use at Locks for fitting bowler hats. A nest of movable rods that finally reproduces the true shape of a head. Every bump. To push them all in until I reach something solid. Round and round, like peeling an onion. Like this . . . like that . . . I hate those phrases. The first try can't be true. Each time plane down another area. As time runs out I need a record. Truth and the ear. The vanity itself part of the fact. The struggle to really get the thing, and not the many neat and true-looking *other* terminations. This is the body of what went on when we met, underneath the words. The real feelings, seasons, weather. The other noises that were more important to me as we talked. To leave myself open, with trust. I shake your hand. And again it is impossible. I know even now there are things I will leave out; things I will distort. But that is also the truth. If the skeleton is false in parts I can't remove or replace them now. Sunlight on the road as she met me that morning. Something she couldn't remember. There was a card from Ron she said. Oh yes she said, he said Frank O'Hara died two days ago.

At least I was never arrested for anything *good*. That month I had to stop myself because I was convinced Americans were incapable of love, listening to them talking to their wives, the same words we use, I couldn't believe it. Because they've never been bombed. That was after I found out Pearl Harbour was on Hawaii, not the mainland, and all the time I'd been giving them credit for that at least. Losing cohesion, my arms and legs slightly out of time. I went to the library and took out three books I already had at home.

There was this man, she said, and, you know, his left eye was somehow turned, all you could see was the red. And at school, when somebody wouldn't share something, cakes, sweets, we'd say Think of Freddy Lane's watery eye when you're eating that.

There were peacocks in Danson Park at the beginning of the war, in an enclosure next to the Olde Englishe Rose Garden. The trams went down to Woolwich, a jumble of tracks at the terminus in the square. Picking my way across them coming home. When they remade the road, after the trolleybuses started, we used the old tarry wood blocks on the fire that winter. Spitting stones across the room as they burned.

'41 or '42. John getting off the train in Wales. Evacuated. In a rage, a cardboard label on his lapel 'To Mrs. Lloyd, George Street, Llanelly'. Get this *off* me ... I'm NOT a PARCEL! And in the night crying I want my mummy. Ken's parents in the East End. Ros always wanted a suitcase. At the camp they went to in the summer all the girls had them. And she just a wicker basket with a lid. Bill wanted long grey socks with coloured bands at the top like the posh kids had. But most of all a pair of shoes. His boots with SHOREDITCH BOROUGH COUNCIL stamped all over them.

Ros wanted to take down the Anderson shelter and undid it from inside. Buried under hundredweights of earth. Ken in the infants' school with his head on his hands staring at another boy and wondering If I blink in time with him now, will we blink in time for ever? Eyes. Years later, I discovered that when he was small Barry used the same method as I to get to sleep. Wet your eyelids with spit, shut your eyes. Then stare through the closed lids at a bright light. That glass bridge at the new school filled with smoke.

I found my mind did not quite control me. On a crowded train for instance, sitting down, a woman standing, I would no longer get up. But my knees would twitch. I didn't really want to stop. Indulged my tempers. Would build them until I could scream, hurl things to the ground, wipe the cups from the table. As I peeled off one skin I retreated further inside. Growing stronger with the concentration. Contemptuous and completely sure of my own position I could not at last be bothered to argue, to listen. Intuition I still believed in above reason. The *feel* of the thing. The oiled way it moved.

The rain did not go. A van passed. I crossed the road. To the left a small square, patch of turf, grey chipped flagstones. Old gravestones trimmed to fit. The light from the office-block shadowed the letters. Mary Hopkins, wife of the above, died August 18th, 1842. One stone, neatly halved, read only June 25th, 1858, aged 2 years and 6 months. The trees were still. No breeze through the city at this time. An occasional newspaper truck. Through the square and into the meat market. 2.30 a.m. Tea and bacon sandwiches. Jerking lights; voices. The noise of frozen carcasses being unloaded was like small explosions. I meant to telephone her.

You see, she said, you don't need me and I don't need you. I moved the receiver to my other ear. So that's it. So. I said So when are we going out again? You can make time. I could hear children playing while I waited for her to answer. Have you got the window open? What? she said. I can hear some kids. God she went on, there's thousands of them. They must breed like rabbits. She giggled. So listen. What are you doing tonight? Look she said, I don't have a minute to spare. I mean you're holding me up now. I got to take things to the cleaners and wash my hair. And two dresses to make by Wednesday or before. Just don't have a minute to spare. I let her talk on. Tomorrow I have to pack. You know *she's* packed already. Then Wednesday I got to take all the bags to the airport. I said You know that plane's going to crash. Don't she said, I've been having dreams about that all week. Right over the Pyrenees I went on. I'll be watching the papers Friday morning. Don't she said again. The children were still there. Love me? No she said. You don't need me, you've got someone. And you've got a nice little feller. Ahhhh she said. You going to write me? No. I won't have the money.

Send you a postcard though. Five words. Look she went on, I'll see you when I get back. If you get back I said. But I guess you'll be packing for next year then. Or something. I mimicked her; I just *got* to get everything done in time. No, not tonight, I have to *baby*-sit. Oh I do love you. Yes I said. I do, but it's not worth it. Yes I said. Look I have to go. Yes I said, I'll see you tomorrow. O.K. Yes. I love you I heard faintly as I put down the receiver. There were small beads of sweat on it as I took my hand away. I wiped my palm on my trousers.

He stood for a while staring through the window, but all he could see was the bright reflection of the room. Pulling the curtains he picked up the phone. Listening to the ring his foot began to itch again. Changing the receiver to his left hand he sat on the arm of the chair, pushed down his sock and began to scratch. The scab was dry. He lifted the edge gently and it came away. Put it in his mouth and tasted the salt. The exchange answered. He gave her name and the Milan number and listened to the noises. First just the sounds of the exchange, then the faint clicks as the operator keyed out the number, a sharp 'ping', a pause, finally the long ringing tone. Which stopped. 'Pronto!' Then nothing more as the operator cut him out of circuit. Then she was there. Pronto he said and she laughed. Gerry! She laughed again. Baby I wish to *christ* I could get out of here he said. How's it been? Listen he went on, it's been believe me a ROUGH, a ROUGH two weeks. But the MONEY baby. Gerry she said, I hope it's all worthwhile. I'm WORKING for a LIVING, o.k.? Let's hope it's all worth-

while has this NEGATIVE bit about it. I mean it's o.k. when
I say it baby. Gerry, you know who I saw here today? The
Evans. Oh no baby he said, the Evans? Well, you know
what I say baby . . . if you're gonna sell out, sell out BIG.
That Evans . . . How the hell can you sell out big in the
POLICE department? I mean if he'd even TRIED he'd be at
least a CAPTAIN. Just don't talk to me about the Evans.
Someone says something obsCENE to her on the phone
and six years later they STILL got an unlisted number
because she's COWering with fear. Where's Vince? she
asked. Vince. . . ? Oh he's gone to some party with this
Martin dame. A bright kid. But I dunno baby. She's the
daughter of some newspaper writer here. Bright . . . you
know . . . but. Few years back she ran off, and for days he
filled the end of his column with Help me find my daughter bits. And they did. In a phone booth shot full of heroin.
Yeh. Sure it's a shame. But not my cup of cunt baby. He
laughed. Not my cup of cunt. No, no . . . it's been quiet
enough. Strangely enough, remarkably enough, I've been
remarkably calm about the whole thing. AND I went
through the whole goddam file . . . seventeen goddam files
in fact. But it's over now. They were downstairs this morning having lox and bagels so I joined them for a coffee.
Then we went up and I guess I had a coupla whisky sours.
Had dinner this evening with Tim Mansky and his wife.
Then back here. Tomorrow I'm off to Frankfurt. So how've
you been? Gerry she said, you know that woman I met in
Egypt? Her boyfriend showed up on his way to Sweden. I
had him over to eat. NICE he said, NICE. So that's it. And
what about that French girl of yours . . . Maureen, wasn't

it? NOT Maureen he said. How the hell could MAUREEN be French? It was Beatrice. Anyway, now she calls herself Michèle. Better than Beatrice. At least she's LEGITI-MATELY French. She said Lively time you're having Gerry. And he began to shout WILL YOU GET IT THROUGH YOUR FUCKING HEAD THAT EVERYTHING IS DULL. ALL THESE PEOPLE AFTER A DAY OR SO BORE THE PISS OUT OF ME. Gerry. Gimme a minute, gimme a minute baby. There's someone at the door. In the distance she heard a girl's voice, then he was back. For Vince he said. Some dame. Just hold on, I better leave him a note. He spelled it aloud as he wrote. F I O N A called 12.15. You get a lot of that? she asked. SURE baby, wadya expect . . . they see in the paper he's here. I'm like the Mother Superior. Know which ones have four month abortions and so on. Listen, you know he has those jazz discs he plays all the time? Well I was here alone yesterday so I went through them. And found a couple of REAL music, not even opened, still in the plastic. So I'm here in the afternoon with a drink, laying down, listening to the Ninth when IN walks this blonde. Stands there, looks at the Hi-Fi, looks at me, pulls the WEIRDEST face you ever saw and walks out again. Thought you were queer and it wasn't worth it she said. And went on Is Maxie still with that woman? Yeah he said. Boy they deserve each other. He's so GODdam tight. At dinner he's all the time looking down the 2/6, 3/6 columns.

∾

His back was to the street and he watched the reflections in a shop window. Olmar left the bank and walked towards his car. As Rinkoff left the doorway he took the gun from his pocket with his right hand, held it by his thigh and cocked it with his left. Movement like pulling on a tight glove. A smear of grease streaked his left index finger. Now he was behind Olmar starting to cross the pavement diagonally towards the car. A little out of breath raising the gun. Olmar was sideways to him now, his right arm outstretched to the door handle. The bullets made small holes in his raincoat. Cigarette smoke trailed from his mouth. The street was still; silent. Olmar fell. Then Rinkoff heard two sounds. The car keys in Olmar's hand scraping the concrete. Himself whistling.

Scragg had an irritating voice. Like a radio tuned slightly off station. The sibilants too loud and long. Have a SWHISTLEleep, he said, or would you rather talk? Shouldn't we be playing draughts? asked Rinkoff. He smiled. Rinkoff smiled. Pleasantly Rinkoff said Open the door you bastard and let me out. Go on he said. Scragg looked nervous. Make a gesture. Be sensible said Scragg, sit down. There was no clock. And neither Scragg nor Murtagh wore watches. Rinkoff was walking up and down. Listen he said, they don't REALLY want to get rid of me. I'm still FULL of ideas. About EVERYTHING. He was rubbing his hands together now. At least give me a chance. Hunt me. Could smear me with fox scent. Drip my blood on babies' faces. Now Scragg looked worried. Watched the door. Rinkoff went to piss. Behind him he heard the door open and crash shut. Murtagh's voice. But he was thinking of Egypt. That day beside the canal. The camel lying on the sand not willing to get up. And the Arab with a wooden beam; nails in the end. SMASH. SMASH on the camel's head. SMASH again. And again. Until it was dead. Just a little too far from the water. The Arab straining to pull, feet slipping in the sand. Then round to the back, pushing. The rear lifting till the legs were straight, then the sudden late working of the camel's bowels. Foul mess over his robe. And already in the water against the low bridge the swollen bodies of two other animals ready to explode. Hairless pink dogs. The flies on children's eyes. He turned round smiling. Can I see the breakfast menu now? he asked. I believe I have a choice. Something constipating I think.

Scragg and Murtagh were pained. This was not how things should be. Rinkoff should be quietly on his mattress, or quietly talking, or quietly writing to his mother. Dear mother, oh mother. I didn't mean to kill Olmar. I thought it was the Woolworth gun I had in my pocket. To frighten him a little. Mother the street was so quiet and cold. Like Christmas morning from midnight mass. My breath made a cloud and my hands were colder in my gloves than out. You see mother his keys scraped the pavement. The cigarette burned a hole in his coat. Mother I am not bad. God will forgive me. The chaplain is a comfort. Scragg and Murtagh are a help in my last hours. They will witness this letter as my own unaided effort so you can sell it to the papers. Buy a cottage in the country with the money.

Move away. How the neighbours must be talking. Mother do you remember the war? The night the bomb dropped. As it exploded you dived with me under the table. Uncle Edward was there as well with his A.R.P. helmet on. He dived for the stairs to the cellar and his head smashed straight into the gas-meter. In the middle of the noise he was silently showered with silver coins. Goodbye mother. I feel it is raining outside today though of course I can't see. Your loving son, Rinkoff.

But he had not written. Nor slept. He had walked and talked. And now walked and talked some more. Sometimes he looked at the other door from the cell. A sound of sawing. Scragg whispered to Murtagh. Speak UP gentlemen said Rinkoff, will you not spend this hour with me? Talk, he said, now. About anything. For instance sex he said, what do you DO? Now Murtagh I always picture in the cinema next to little girls. His raincoat over his knees, hand sliding onto their legs. A lover of gym-slips, of navy blue knickers. And Scragg? I see him on his days off standing staring at the cards. RUBBER RAINWEAR A SPECIALITY. FOUNDATIONS, ERECTIONS, DEMOLITIONS, MISS C. VERE. 40 INCH CHEST — RING ANY TIME. YOUNG LADY SEEKS PART TIME WORK IN CONGENIAL POSITION. Or writing off for lists of photographs. SET 1. Come and see dark-haired curvaceous Françoise. Françoise this voluptuous french chick is not very chic as she is unusually LARGE with a 46 inch bust which is well rubbed-in with oil to highlight her grotesque bosom. The lens on the cameras steams up every time Françoise pouts challengingly at you to dare defy her charms. Now Rinkoff paced the room. SET 2. FLAME CORBETT: This collection is not for men . . . only for HE-men! Better be fireproof, 'cos when she performs (she's not bashful) you'll smoulder and cringe for mercy when you see her shaking her fabulous 44 : 23 : 39. Complete set of eight studies. Shall I go on Scragg? Do you have those in your collection Scragg? LISTEN TO ME SCRAGG as Scragg stared red and angry at the floor. Rinkoff lay down on his mattress. You think I should be scared he said to them. So do I. But I can't manage it. He looked at the broken skin around his thumbnail.

What can I do? he said. What can I talk to you about?

You see he went on, something always happens. Let me explain. Have you never walked across a bridge and THOUGHT about it. While you're standing there, in the middle, above the deepest water. And you realise that you, there, could unthink that bridge if the right gears in your brain would mesh. You stand on that structure of spaces and don't fall through. You could do it but there's a block. That's how I feel now. I'll get up in a moment. Something will make contact.

Now he said to them, the hangman is having supper with the Governor. Off willow-pattern plates with shapeless cutlery. The Governor's wife has arranged the flowers. Perhaps she had a headache and will go to bed. And they will get a little drunk and talk. The lights here never go

[16]

out. He thought of China. The time passed. It must be nearly ready he said. There was no change in the lighting. Murtagh pushed back his cuff, then remembered. Voices now in the next room. Breakfast.

Rinkoff asked for more eggs, then pissed again. The chaplain came in. A bell rang somewhere . . . Seconds Out. Green sleep in the corner of the chaplain's left eye. He tried to pick it out with his left middle finger nail, the book in his right hand. Scragg and Murtagh were standing now. Rinkoff began to giggle. He walked towards the other door. Opening. Rinkoff passed through. The room was black.

And until that point I had never really intended to write the truth. I took the book from my case (remembering again as I saw the towel, the edge of another book, that she had not made the sandwiches; but with some affection) and began. For a while I couldn't think, not think where I was, where I was going. Was not sure if I had only thought the thing, or done it. But I was on the train. People got up and moved to the door. A man who looked like Bob Brown, with glasses, a thick black Crombie overcoat with a half-belt. A woman in a blue coat, with fair hair. Opposite me an old woman with sour mouth reading a paper, the end of it hanging over her knees. Behind me two people talking about leukaemia. Again I was swallowing the truth, burying it under those details.

I looked further back in the book. And read. Realised that

while it was possibly a dam that might be blown up, and which *could* be holding back a great flood of water, equally the channel might be dry, bottom cracked. The effect would be the same. It was easy to produce clever little exercises, puns, twistings of words, while it was nearly impossible to capture any emotion or feeling. Then when I started I had all those years of I I I ME ME to wash out. Like the rusty water from the tap at first in a long-empty house.

I am typing at the table, now 1960. Over the carriage and the paper I can look out, through net curtains, at the road; the houses opposite. Not directly out, but slightly up; we are living in a sub-basement. To the left stairs, or rather steps, slant up to the street. Where they flatten at the top stand three empty milk bottles. Between them and the pavement is an iron railing that tilts to the right. Directly ahead is the garden. One plant growing straight up out of a mixture of wild grass and yellow flowers that can only be weeds. There are more bottles in the grass, bits of newspaper, one or two tins. Odd bits of rubbish that have drifted there from the three dustbins, out of sight, hidden by the steps leading down from the front door. Between the garden and the road, a brick wall. Over the wall the top 1½ floors of the houses across the street. The roofs of cars as they pass. Heads of people. The whole framed by three trees; one to my left (close) and two over the road. A continuous noise of traffic, not heavy, just the sound of one car passing at a time, nearly dying away before the next. The clatter of a load shifting on a truck as it goes round the bend. Black tiles on the roofs opposite. There is a noise of wind in the trees. Three matchsticks and a Cadbury chocolate wrapper lie just outside the window on the bricks that border the path. A woman shouts Joan . . . JOAN . . . if he comes let him in . . . the door's open . . . I got no key. She wheels a baby round to the right. Stops. Comes back to pick up the pram pillow.

∾

My father died / I closed his eyes / outside the cabin door. / The lawyer and the sheriff / had been the day before. His mother would sing in the kitchen. Let my loving wife / neither weep nor sigh. / For Ireland's sake / I am proud to die. She would be singing all day. She is far from the land / where her young hero sleeps / and lovers around her are sighing. / But coldly she turns / from their gaze and weeps / for the heart of the minstrel is crying. He didn't remember the songs correctly, neither did she, bits she filled in with humming. The history of Ireland he knew before he went to school. First in every Gaelic kingdom came the highest of grades, of rulers, churchmen, and poets. From Fionn, who when he was grown went to study poetry under the old druid Finegas. For seven years Finegas had been trying to catch the salmon of knowledge in the river Boyne. So one day he caught it and told Fionn to roast it for him. You didn't eat any? he asked when it was brought to him. No said Fionn, but I burned my thumb on it and put it in my mouth. Then said the druid sadly, it's you and not I who will be wise. Through Emmett, who would never have been caught but for his love for Sarah Curran. Instead of escaping he went back to see her. Let no man write my epitaph he said. Hanged drawn and quartered. And when they held up his head in St. Thomas Street in the hush the only sound was of a locket falling from his neck. And in it a strand of hair from Sarah Curran. Up to Connolly and the GPO. So the English took him out, on the stretcher, tied him to a chair to keep him upright, and shot him. When he was seven he went with his parents to Dublin. St. Stephen's Green. Eden Quay. Oh the moon shines tonight along the Liffey / where the heroes of Sinn Fein in ambush lay. / May they rest in peace those men who died for Ireland / on the banks of the Liffey, Eden Quay. He never got the whole story from her, and never asked. His grandparents were there in O'Casey's book. Mr. Moore walking bareheaded in the pouring rain at his wife's funeral. The least I can do for her he said. An old letter he found from an uncle in Australia. Saying I am enclosing the form and would be glad if you would get it sent along to Sean Price or Frank Daly to fill in as I have forgotten the dates. I have written to Sean McEntee about being arrested in the tunneling into Mountjoy Jail.

He remembered his father going when he was two. Just an image of a rifle leaning against a chair in the back room. And being held up to wave as someone went round the corner. He had many memories of infant school. A boy, Michael, they must both have been about five, playing in the yard. Michael had taken up a small grille covering a drain, put one foot in, watched the water swell out, then put in the other and stuck. Had started crying; the older girls had come around (until the age of six the boys played in the girls' yard) but no-one did anything. He had tried to lift him out, and not knowing how, in some panic, Michael screaming now, had taken him with both hands around the neck and tried to lift, not understanding, trying to pull him up until at last the teacher, a nun, had come and pulled him away, beating him for hurting poor Michael. Later when he was seven, drawing on brown paper with square powdery crayons he had sucked the end of one. And a different teacher had pulled him to the front of the class shouting You naughty boy WHY have you EATEN a crayon? And he denied it saying I did NOT eat a crayon. And she said LOOK at your mouth . . . COVERED in it. The situation developing to where she would have him admit he had eaten a crayon, eaten for her meaning merely placed in the mouth. And he refusing, eaten for him meaning to chew and swallow. His mother coming to collect him that evening being told He is a STUBBORN CHILD my dear, you must PRAY for him.

There were no mad men now on the streets, the harmless ones that would walk down the middle of the road, their hair long. The man in plusfours always waving his walking stick in the air and shouting at shopkeepers. His wife had told him how she once worked in a library with a girl who had a club foot. Until one night she had dreamed she was in the basement and the girl was coming slowly down the stairs. First one foot, then bringing the other down to it, then one foot again. And she knew she was coming to kick her, to kick her to death with that foot. And in Wales there had been a madman living next door to her, not violent, but they'd taken him away. Three years later he'd been released. Nose flat to his face broken many times; around his eyes masses of scars. Then he had a 'relapse' and his wife called for them to come and get him. And he had jumped the garden fence, come into their house and clung to her grandfather's knees, begging him not to let them take him, until her grandfather also was crying, holding him. But he was taken back of course, and died there a month later. Her grandmother in that same town having her first child at nineteen. And wondering why it always cried. Nursing it for weeks until it died. And then the doctors examining it and saying it had been born with a broken back; had been in agony all those weeks. So even now she was terrified whenever anyone was pregnant.

The things they had done that they would never dare now. He at ten exploring inside a drain for miles under the town, and somehow coming back the right way to the open exit in the park. (The water flowing into the lake, the couples in their boats rowing around the island.) She at the same age rowing across the deep dock on a piece of corrugated iron. The industries dead then in that town, the harbour silting up, rail tracks through the streets covered in grass, empty steelworks. Down by the dock a whole street of public houses run by retired sea-captains. Her grandfather could remember them; a parrot in every window. Now closed and shuttered. Or turned into fish and chip shops. At the end of the street the bleak Baptist chapel.

It was a release to write it down. Slipping from I to he. From he to I. Traffic moved past the window, noisier now in the evening, the children quiet, no sounds of cooking, the air cold in the room. The yellow light from the street lamp blurring on the dirty window pane. On the white wall a child's handprint, marks of their pencils. In the kitchen a line of measurements and dates. So many things

to talk about with friends. Whole evenings to be spent
on food, on films, the war. Ration books she would say,
do you remember? Those cheap paper pages with the
fibres showing. The little squares marked eggs; meat;
cheese. Checked off each week with a long blue tick. The
sweet coupons you cut out, small as a postage stamp, and
held tight all the way to the shop. Once we had a whole
bunch of bananas she said, my uncle was in the Merchant
Navy. The queues for oranges. Over in the park, beside the
empty swimming pool, the anti-aircraft guns. After the
war the vacant sites used for cycle speedway. The Welling
Wheels. Lowgeared bikes with high forked handlebars.
Two streets away more guns dug in on a road island. The
barrage balloons on their long cables. At night the noise,
the mattress on the dining room table. They slept underneath. The names of the shelters: Anderson, the one dug
deep in the garden and roofed with corrugated iron and
sandbags. Morrison, the one in a room, like a table made
of iron girders and wire mesh. You were supposed to sleep
inside it every night. Watching the water run downstairs
when the shrapnel ripped through the tank. And all that
summer filling in the crater with rubbish. Derek still
keeping the tattered label marked dead in pencil that
they'd put round his neck when they pulled him out. The
artificial pools made of brick all over the town filled with
water for the firemen. And left so long after the war two
children he knew drowned in them. Public shelters still
standing then as well. Smells of dog and old bits of newspaper in the corners. Where he had his first kiss from
Frances Debney after school. The German plane brought

down a few streets away. The British bomber crash-landed in the park, left there for a week for people to look at, touch, walk inside. Cramped even for him as he bent to get in. How could men fly in it? The funny little letters from his father. Thin things, reduced photographs of letters written on official forms. Thick black lines added by the censor. And all the time the sirens. Later the doodlebugs. You could hear them coming. Even see them, their funny tails. They passed over and the engine stopped. Everyone would watch as they began to glide down. If they cut out directly above you you were safe, they'd land miles away. Then in the last months the rockets. Dear Werner. He would always remember the bright flash and the house on the hill vanishing. And the noise of that very advanced, faster than sound rocket coming after the explosion.

So many things they had almost stopped talking about the future. They would start, but the conversation would bend and bend until again they were talking about Madelaine Carroll, whatever happened to Richard Conte? I used to LOVE John Garfield, Deanna Durbin, Margaret Lockwood. Scenes recalled from old films, separately, or pieced together between them. Mikes would bring cakes for the children who would go into the garden with cream around their mouths while more tea was made and they sat in the kitchen in the evenings talking, always talking.

When people came sometimes his wife wouldn't think, would bring them in, go to him and he would curse her, tell her to go back, to tell them he wasn't in, sick, all the time knowing that he would soon go into the room. They would be sitting on the couch facing the door, would smile, get up, shake his hand, sit down. He would light a cigarette and it would begin all over again. Sometimes the children would come in, the girl peering round the door always carrying something. The boy, talking more, with some excuse to speak to his mother. And the visitors would look at the children and smile, say How many have you got? Oh isn't he, she, it SWEET, DO let us see the baby. And to the end he would be polite, give them books, refuse the money, take their addresses, phone numbers. Perhaps one or two a year would become friends and after two or three years he could even talk to them.

'The war in Munster continued, but John Fitzgerald was killed in 1582 and the Geraldines soon lost heart. It was said that the lowing of a cow or the voice of a ploughman could not be heard from Cashel to the furthest point of Kerry. The poor Earl of Desmond offered to surrender on terms, but no terms would be given him. At last in the winter of 1583 he was tracked down to a small hut near Tralee—betrayed by a kinsman of his own. A soldier breaking into the hut found a man with snow-white hair, feeble and wasted with suffering who cried Spare me, I am the Earl of Desmond. But the soldier killed him with a blow of his sword; the Desmond estates were declared forfeit to the crown.'

~

After Anselm and Josie left ('65) we put the children to bed. I moved the chairs and table. We pulled out the couch and made the bed. Left the washing up till the morning. I lay there, thinking as usual about this, working out how I would write it, certain ideas came. It was raining outside, a windy night, the trees moving. I thought about it. How it should start where I was lying in bed thinking about it and then GOT UP and did it. Right I thought, I'll get up. In some way make myself MOVE after the last three years. And immediately thought I'd go to sleep and do it in the morning. But fake it. Write it as though I HAD got up. Put it off a little further. Perhaps even be honest at the end, a twist. I didn't get up and begin. Or what? The weight of the three years, all the times I didn't move, had the paper, the time, but wrote on envelopes, bus tickets, was there, with the thought, didn't do it. Didn't move.

What happened in those three years? Four years ago I had the energy. Worked, came home, set type, put type back in the case, went to bed at three, got up at six, carried the type to work with me, in the evening printed two pages. Met people, telephoned, wrote letters. How did it all drain away? Three years ago I slowed, two years ago I made a few jerks, one year ago I stopped.

If this is to be the form I should name the names. Put it together yourself. Fit the pieces. Make me work. Of the people I met from that time and before who remain? Anselm and Josie Hollo, Ed & Helene Dorn, Ken & Pat

Lansdowne, Mike Horovitz, Piero Heliczer, Dave and Nicole Ball. A few others. Most, in their way, went. Certainly there was enough kindness there at particular times. I was sane during this period and they knew where I was in their patterns. But I wanted to find out. Where I am. Most loved me like a dog; I was forgiven my small lapses.

I can remember all that time. You name it. It's there. The day I went to Piero's wedding. Chelsea Town Hall. I can tell you. That morning I went to the grocers. We were living in Amhurst Road, Hackney. On the way back I passed a policeman on a grey horse. By two o'clock I was late and took a taxi. The driver was bald and the number of the cab was 6954. I'd borrowed an old camera from Sid Fletcher and worried that I mightn't be able to work it. As the taxi turned into Park Lane the sun came out and the camera slid along the seat. Piero arrived first, a wilting sprig of marijuana in his lapel. Then Kate in another taxi. The registrar queried her name and asked her mother what she called her. I call her lots of things she said. The sun came through the window.

Or did it begin listening to Jimmy Yancey playing 'How Long Blues'? Maybe it started there in Alec's front room (1956). His mother would bring us in tea and they had an old oil stove that burned with a red flame. Or even with his sister. I fancied her, and to keep us from going out I used music. I would play his piano, made him buy a clarinet, Dave a trumpet. Last time I saw him, '60 or '61, he was playing clarinet in the Fireman's Band. We would play records, those old Vogue 78's with the red labels. Gillespie's 'The Champ' . . . R & B—'Good Mornin' Judge' . . . 'Don't Roll those Bloodshot Eyes at Me'. Bright summer evenings I would walk to his house; always a faint smell of burning wood. Sometimes she would answer the door.

'Have him' Joe said (1957). The windows were misted with steam and Les was serving hot sausage sandwiches. He was sitting there at the end table with three friends. We watched him. Flash cunt Don said. You load SIXteen tons went the record. He avoided looking at us, tapping his spoon on his saucer, smiled, said something to the others. CUNT Joe said, Look at him. I went into the yard at the back to piss. Listened to it wash across the empty bottles. They went out, past the post office (Frances Debney's road), we followed. Lights still on in Woolworth's window; a bus moving up the hill. WHAT d'you GET he was singing slapping his hands against his trousers. They went into the toilet next to the library. Hey Joe said and pulled his shoulder. Hey again. He turned, still holding his cock and Joe hit him in the stomach. The other three ran out. He bent forward and the back of his jacket was soaked as the toilet flushed. I leaned against the radiator and watched. Same radiator I'd warmed myself against one November morning after a night sleeping in a broken down Ford in the car park. A Sunday morning. Later from Les's window I'd watched my parents turning the corner opposite on their way to mass. Oh mother he was shouting, help me. And Don kicked his leg as he started to run. He stumbled, kept going, got through the door and we watched him go down the street. Mother help me he was still shouting and his three friends were standing in a shoeshop doorway looking at him. A car passed. A trolleybus turned the corner.

Firm between your fingers, soft between your lips . . . or something like that would go the advert. Like a PRICK Dave would shout and we'd be barred from another cinema. I recognise you, you with that blond hair the manager would say, You're BARRED for LIFE! And he would brace back his scruffy evening jacket and we would go to the park those summer nights, sit on the kids' swings and watch the idiots go by.

But our first and only concert was a mess. My piano was all right hand and hit a few clumps of notes every now and then with the left. Dave's trumpet was imitation Chet Baker, and John's drums were straight from lesson six at the Bexleyheath School of Dance Music. Do you ever see John now? I asked Colin (1962). Oh, he's playing the boats now, and Janie's gone back to her mother with the kid. She was tall, very thin, and fair. Nick me a felt typewriter pad to practice on he asked then. It's all in the wrist Frankie Machine I said and hit his arm. But we did at least play that Working Men's Club. Two numbers. Sometimes I saw Alec's sister going to work. But now I had a strange girl from a convent who pressed her stomach against me when we danced and worried about me. I don't remember her name, but one evening she wore a pink hat and I couldn't see her again after that. We're going to invade Egypt Mike said in the Embassy Ballroom. And I lost ten shillings betting he was wrong through not reading the papers. She left the hat in the cloakroom but it was too late. Sometimes they would laugh in the wrong place, or sneeze, or move awkwardly in the rain and it would be over. Help me he screamed and tried to button his trousers as he ran.

Now 1945. My father went when I was two and came back one night when I was seven. My mother let me stay up and I lay on the cold couch in the front room by the fire, later and later. Finally I went to sleep. Suddenly there was noise. I woke up. It was bright. Spit had run out of my mouth and left a dark patch on the cushion. There was a tall thin man in uniform with my mother. A dark brown face. Through the open street door I could see a trolley, the sort you find on stations, loaded with kitbags. It was freezing. He had come from Burma to London in November, but Army Regulations had somehow insisted that overcoats be handed in at the docks. Those same regulations I heard more about from Bert Swanwick (1958) when he was talking about the 1st World War. Of his company, only fifty men had been left. Captured by the Germans they were put to work first in the mines, then, happily, in a vineyard for the rest of the war. The night he was captured his hair turned white. In 1918, when they got back to England, every one of them had the value of their lost equipment deducted from their back pay. My father had arrived at one in the morning. No transport at that time, a friendly porter had lent him the station trolley to carry his bags. Now he had to take it back to the station. Home for one week, he was sick with bronchial pneumonia and spent the next six in the military hospital. All I remember there is one ward filled with German prisoners of war, with armed sentries at the door. They made beautiful wooden toys for our Christmas Bazaar.

My mother being Irish, a catholic from birth, there was no real zeal behind her religion. A thing you just did. If you missed mass one sunday, God would understand. Her conversation was sprinkled with God Willing's . . . Jesusmaryandjosephprotectus she would say as the bombs fell. In 1964, when we were in real trouble, evicted from our flat, no money, my wife and I went down to see her. Without thinking, after hearing the story, my mother said Ah well, God is good. But my father was a convert, with the missionary fervour. He could never see how I could so easily throw away something it had taken him thirty years to reach.

~

It was a bad picture, but suddenly the word 'frontier' made him cry. There was a foreign name that made him cry also. He wore sun glasses and did not take them off during the interval. He began to cry again during the main film, although the girl reminded him of no-one he knew; she had dark hair and was young. Outside, the cars were parked on both sides of the road. Engines started and lights came on. People were eating expensive cakes in the coffee bar. He did not know why he had cried, though 'frontier' seemed a reasonable thing to cry at. At night the searchlights flickered along each strand.

Between the first and last time he went there was a period of two or three weeks when he did not think much about it. That final time he stood by the wall and watched them. He drank, but nothing happened. The man who spoke to him was polite but he was as rude as he could think and went out to the hall. A beer bottle foamed over and soaked his trousers, then he felt a little better. One of the girls had warm hair and her top teeth stuck out. Her dress had three pleats down the back, and she danced with someone else but looked at him when he wasn't watching her. They all danced, but every three minutes the record had to be changed. Photographs were stuck to the wall in some kind of pattern. One of a sad girl with dark hair. The lights were dim and the lino brown. The people did not quite cover all the empty space.

From the balcony he sighted an imaginary rifle at a man in the stalls. Told his friends how only last week a balcony had collapsed and they all laughed. This time he did not wear his sun-glasses because the doctor had given him black and green pills which he was to take four times a day. These pills made him feel calmly insane. Behind the school the clock on St. Paul's chimed six times.

He sat on the bed for ten minutes telling the child outside how to shut the door Turn the handle and PULL knowing all the time it was too stiff for her.

Always as she talked she moved her hands. He caught them and held them tight. Say something he said. She tried and then stopped; he could feel her fingers moving inside his palms. Everything was clear that morning and it took a long while to get the powder and the taste from his mouth.

≈

The room is completely dark. Even my infra-red sensitive eyes see nothing. And there are no sounds. I sit and think. The batteries planted deep within my chest last for 50 years. With the tungsten-tipped drill that is now my left index-finger I could no doubt bore through the wall. But they are waiting for me to make a move. They want to see my power. Just sit and wait. Let them make the moves. This is the final test. Everything must be natural. I need no sleep, but every twelve hours — or rather not exactly twelve, that would be too obvious, more irregular, sometimes after eighteen, sometimes after eight — I lie on the bed. It's then I hear small sounds, clicks, scratchings. My eyes pick out the warm shape of a hand, low down, near the floor. And then there is food. Which I eat, use, and excrete. My whole training has been for this moment. Long ago, when I had real hands, eyes, before the operations, the thin wires, the delicate bondings of metal and plastic to flesh, the protection or replacement of my organs, my beautiful stomach that can detect and alter poisons and chemicals, I knew this. And knew that I would be the first. Through my memory I play the Mozart flute quartet in A. And remember. Did I ever get the secret I was sent for? It's not important for me to know. If I did, it's safe on tape and film somewhere inside. I tap my chest and feel the steel under the soft covering. Hear the faint sound. I am the secret marvel of the age. They allow me to be proud. Everything, every part of me that could be changed or improved, mechanically or electronically, has been. Delicate screens drop and lift inside my eyes; with different fingers I can shoot, drill, turn screws, file. I breathe, and the chemicals and gases are used more purely than before. My heart beat is regular and can never stop. And I am still human because I know all this and can remember before. Before, when what I was, when my humanity, or human-ness, was a drawback to my profession. When I was weak, destructible. When my sole defense against torture, against drugs, was myself. How could I function, how could they trust me with a factor inside that no-one could determine? They removed my right arm first, and when I woke I could do the same things, and *more* with the new one. I hear the smallest sound, scent the faintest odour. I remember high above the city at night in a small room pulling back the curtains, pigeon-droppings on the balcony, how I stared for the first time with my new eyes across the street and into the dark room opposite with curtains drawn. And as I watched the shapes moving, and recognised them, I knew I should cry, and tears came. I knew I should stop, and they stopped.

He opened the door of his room and grinned at me. Spoke my name and led me in, one arm around my shoulders, squeezing. Noticing nothing, he poured me a drink, asked if I had eaten. I kept the volume of my voice down, controlled, answered his questions. He looked the same but I knew he had erred. We make no mistakes. On the table a litter of papers, pens, glue. Full ashtrays. A lamp at an angle still burning. Each time there was a pause in the conversation he looked at me and smiled. I told him of my travels. He went into the kitchen to get more ice and

I began to burn his papers. Smelling the smoke he came back, asked what I was doing, pushing against me, trying to put out the flames with his hands. I caught and squeezed them. Tightened my grip until the fingers broke and blood squirted from under his nails. Until a high note came from his mouth. Lifting him into a chair I went on with my work. Pulling open drawers, cupboards, I burned everything. Then he tried to shoot me, pain on his face as he tried to steady the gun. And watching his eyes, making no move, I saw his mind crack as the bullet struck my forehead and fell to the ground. I opened the end of my finger and fired once; noise like someone spitting. The flames rose. On top of the pile a photograph bent and melted round the edges. A picture, underexposed, of two people smiling at the camera, arm in arm on a pavement somewhere. Louise and me. I remembered.

The sun was at that particular winter angle and intensity when everything appears artificially lit. Cars ticked past. Walking slowly in the sunlight we fumbled crossings, not sure if cars would stop or turn. Hearing non-existent noises and reacting nervously. We had just left the room (his shoes are melting now, the fat on his legs crackling).

I had gone there early in the morning. The Mozart quartet was playing and I was hungry, had eaten nothing, drunk only strong coffee. I was susceptible, near to tears, feeling dizzy when I smoked. Taking her hand I moved it in time to the music. The gravel in the cement of the balcony flickered in the light as though it were raining. I was

[37]

happy then. What are you doing? she said, to me? and turned. I kissed her without thinking. The thin material of her dressing gown. Pressing her knees and breasts against me hard, but where I felt it was in my stomach where we touched lightly. I sat on the folding bed under the bookcase and read 'Billy the Kid' while she made more coffee in the kitchen, moving the curtain back several times to look at me. "And the day, a hot summer day, with birds in the sky."

I cannot drown. I am shockproof, fireproof, and immune to disease. I believe in what we do. I speak many languages. Air hostesses of all nationalities have served me and remember my face. I am in here, somewhere, feeling the bit turn in the brickwork. Covered with a hard surface of purpose. They cannot reach me. Suspecting I am only a machine they are afraid to dissect me because of the secret. "Torture gardens and scenic railways." I go where they send me. To destroy or steal. To use or persuade. We went to the park and lost our way. Came out of a different exit and walked in the wrong direction.

I was living then in a small flat on the fourth floor of an old six-storey building. The money I had would have lasted about six months. No plans for when it ran out except to get some more. Each morning, from that day, I would get up at eight, make the bed, sweep, wash, drink one cup of whiskey and one of coffee. At a quarter to nine I would lock the door, go down the 72 stairs, check if there was any mail, light a cigarette and walk to her room. Each morning I would pass the same people going to work; the same cafes would be opening. I lost track of the date, but not of the days of the week. Each day at the same time I would climb the wooden stairs, go along the corridor and knock on the door. To the right was the bed, and in front the window which was always open. We talked to each other.

This was the letter I didn't write. Between and around the lines of my formal notes, the requests for you to send me books, to telephone my friends. What I wanted to explain. What I wanted to explain was that my emotions were hanging loose. Like tentacles ready to catch on to anything, to anyone. I could never have left you for any reason. Because all those people I hated would have pitied you and that could never have been true. You were always a person. There at least my ethics worked. And the thoughts of those people concerning you were important to me. Their stupid voices and concern. Their conclusions. Their sympathy leaking out all over you and their secret smugness. Their quiet desperate marriages they would have seen as justified and lasting. I was not aware, and still find it impossible to be, of doing anything wrong. My life takes place from minute to minute. It expands through the gaps that people make. If there is something warm there I sense it. If there is a weakness in the wall I must push through. But no danger exists for you because on the other side are always more walls to explore for cracks. And that is the tension I need to work. Emotion and strain. My disease is the exercise of power *with* feeling for the person. And all this you know and understand already. And I know that. The base is firm, although the trouble and pain are true. Which is why at the same time as I can be thinking of leaving, I wake in the night sweating and worrying if you are not there. Not even a proof of needing. If I am away for a week, for a month, I may only think of you twice. Somewhere inside me is a sick core that knows nothing is important. The dead center *is* dead. Which is what makes it easy to cry as the plague spreads. There is a cruelty in me that I cannot curb which operates only on those who offend my feelings of what they should sense. Who never feel atmosphere, the tension behind words. Who say the phrases that never ring true. And that comes from an exaggerated sense of the importance of my own awareness. I mean, you've just left me with nothing he said. A contemptuous weapon to use. Like saying You wouldn't hit me, would you, I'm a cripple? Why not? No two people are evenly matched in violence, and who can decide what weapons shouldn't be used? The object is to win, not to lose gracefully. There is a correct time. In love all actions are love. *This* is what they don't see. They only understand it as something pleasant that is stopped or upset by certain actions. Because you are so much me I can disregard you as I do parts of my own personality. The networks of lies are as deceptive as acid. The religion behind it all. Whatever you see, wherever you are, you come back to this reality because *here* is where you die. The words I say to you are meaningless, but you sense the truth behind them. I love you in such a way that I can't imagine life without you *somewhere*, even away from me.

How I criticise you and tear at you is *self*-destruction, not simply carping. Do you really believe in sweetness and light, a regular allowance for clothes, a constant stream of darlings and smiles? To force me to build a wall, to force me to make a second, a third secret life. *That* plants the seed of destruction. I sit here now, this Saturday in 1967, drinking whiskey after whiskey, smoking cigarette after cigarette, seeing the form of this book, listening to the children shouting in the garden. Surrounded by possessions. When we moved first, everything we had fitted into the back of a taxi. Two rooms at the bottom of Haverstock Hill. A Put-U-Up with a broken leg. I was always depressed because I had no letters. And the man in the room above had mail every morning marked URGENT. His name was Christopher Brown. And one morning there was a letter from you marked in red 'MORE URGENT THAN CHRISTO-PHER BROWN'S'. What am I doing? Writing about the chances we don't take. And then I find it is about you; the way you bend the lines like a magnet. I put myself in a transparent box, to be attacked from any angle. If our first concert had been a success what could have happened? Who would have been in the box, in the dark room, and why would he have thought he was there?

'Malcolm X's hand flew to his chest as the first of sixteen shotgun pellets or revolver slugs hit him. Then the other hand flew up. The middle finger of the left hand was bullet-shattered, and blood gushed from his goatee. He clutched his chest. His big body struck the stage floor with a thud ... In Long Island, where she had been taken after her father's murder, six year old Attilah carefully wrote a letter to him. "Dear Daddy, I love you so. O dear, O dear, I wish you wasn't dead."'

≈

Perhaps it's therapy. They have put me in here to find myself. I remember the breakdown; the confusion. Skiffle when we started. Or that's what we used to get a hall to practice in. Dave had a friend who played the washboard. Who had some connections with the Boy Scouts and was able to get us the use of their hall every Saturday. A mixed group: piano, trumpet, drums and washboard. We played 'Take the "A" Train' and 'Georgia'. Tried to play 'Night in Tunisia'. Then one evening we found some sound equipment under the stage. A microphone that we connected up to the speakers round the hall. And for the first time I heard my voice amplified, echoing from the walls. So I gave up the piano. Never really liked it; too much to think about with both hands working at the same time. All those progressions, just banging them down while the others improvised. And I always wanted to be in front. So I left Dave and John, and the washboard player. And moved on.

Or when I was seventeen. Another path. Joe and Don. The Sunday evenings in the cinema watching old Warner Brothers gangster films. The sombrely moving cars, sudden noises of gunfire that wakened memories. Joe was the oldest, then about 22. Thin, stupid, and mad about guns. When they finally caught him, under the floorboards of his room they found two sten-guns, five revolvers, a rifle and two automatics. We used to go shooting rabbits down at Gravesend with one of the sten-guns. They disintegrated when you hit them. I was nearly eighteen.

The first job we did together was an Estate Agents. A friend had an aunt working there, and she told him a house had been bought for cash one Saturday afternoon and they hadn't had time to bank the money. We met at the dance-hall with a vague idea of establishing some sort of alibi. At eight-thirty we left, stole a van from the car park (the only motor with the keys left in it) and drove there. The office was on the main road, and the lights were on all night. Parked the van in a side street and went down the road at the back. A narrow lane along the rear of the building. We counted off the windows. Pitch black. Don went over the wall first while Joe and I crouched down behind it. Silence. Ten minutes passed and Joe got nervous. Let's go he said. Don't be a cunt I told him, what about Don? Leave him he said. I shoved him. Do what? What if he had some sort of accident in there? You want us just to piss off and leave him? Get over there and see what's happening. He went over the wall. I waited. Five minutes. Then a crash of breaking glass. I started to walk away, but no-one came, nothing moved. So I went back and climbed over. Reached the back of the office, avoided pieces of broken glass on the ground and climbed in. Don and Joe were in the back room looking at the safe. What happened? I asked Don. I get here, he said, I take out the pane all carefully, I lay it down, then what does this four-eyed git do but come trampling along like a fucking elephant and walks straight over it. Joe blinked. Prick I said to him. He blinked again. And look at *this* fucking thing Don went on, pointing at the safe. It was immense. Until that moment I'd not really thought about it. Had

[44]

imagined it as something about the size of a biscuit tin that we could cart out to the van and crack later. But it looked larger than a fridge. One keyhole and a handle. Well we're not going to open *that* Don said, unless we shove this cunt's thin head in the crack and use him as a fucking lever. He nodded at Joe, who was trying to lift an enormous adding machine from one of the desks. We can get a fiver for this he said. Don pushed him. You tiny-minded bastard that's just about your mark. You think I want to risk two years for a fucking glorified abacus? Joe stared at him. You think you're really hard he said, if I had my shooter here you wouldn't be so bleedin flash. Piss off I told him, I bet you stand in front of the mirror every night waving it about and thinking you're Dillinger. Oh you two piss me off he said, always bleedin nagging. Then I lost my temper. Stamped on his foot, and as he bent, knee'd him in the mouth. Two of his teeth came out and my leg began to bleed. Fucking HELL Don said, where the fuck do you think you are? We'll have the law round before we've even nicked a pencil. O.K. I said. And helped Joe up. You SHIT he kept saying, what you do THAT for? Don was moving around the room; it must have been the manager's office. We can take these . . . he pointed to two small typewriters. And that cigarette box, that lighter. Have a look through the desk. I did. There were a couple of paper knives, a stapler, some other odds and ends. You want to try that? I asked, pointing at the safe. I did he said, it's locked well enough. We couldn't open it. Even from the back? He shook his head. Maybe if we had the tools and more time. But not after all that row. Better take what we can and go. Look for your teeth I said to Joe. If the law finds them they'll use them as evidence. If they can bear to touch them said Don. We left and drove back. Dropped Joe near the dance-hall. Arranged to meet him in the morning to sell the stuff to a dealer in Woolwich. What shall we do? Don asked, I don't feel much like going home. Nor me. Let's have a motor somewhere. We can put this back in the morning.

We drove along the Rochester By-pass. I'd known Don about a year then. Met him through a girl I was going out with called Millett. She had an elder sister, Jackie. Millett was always telling me how great this Jackie's boy-friend Don was. He was doing his National Service in the army; had deserted three times and was at that time in the Army Prison at Shepton Mallet. One evening Millett didn't show up. I went round to her house and she was there with Jackie and Don. I thought you'd come if I wasn't there, she said, so it seemed a waste of time to go out and come back. I knew you'd want to meet Don. The two girls lived with their parents. Their mother was fine, but from all accounts their father a swine. And he hated Don, who had no regular place to stay. If he'd seen him he would have turned him over to the M.P.'s. Each night Don would hide in the playing fields near the house. When her parents were asleep Jackie would open the downstairs window, lock the inside door. He'd climb in and they'd sleep on the couch. Each morning at six he'd leave before anyone woke. Don was the most generous person I ever met. He'd give anything away, down to his last cigarette. And the most vicious fighter. It was from him I learned to always strike the first blow when the tension mounts . . . and once that's done, to never relax the pressure.

We kept driving until the petrol gauge showed half-full then turned back. Early morning now, hardly any traffic. A few lorries in lay-bys. One or two transport cafés open. What you going to do when they call you up? he asked. Dunno. Just go I suppose. You're a cunt if you do he said. Shit-horrible little gits telling you what to do all the time. Clean this polish that come here go there. Lie on your bunk at night and count the days. And I was keen to go in. Thought I'd be a driver. Get abroad somewhere and tear about in one of those enormous great trucks. So I put in for the R.A.S.C. and what happens? They tell me I'm colour blind. And I'd thought they were supposed to find that out at your medical. Colour blind I said . . . fucking charming. Now he tells me. After driving me about all night. It don't make any difference he shrugged. I can figure out the traffic lights. I mean it's only top middle and bottom. Don't really matter what *colours* I think they are. We turned a corner and started up the hill to Sidcup. Right at the top the engine stalled. Outside the police station. Don revved and revved. Deafening. I sat watching the door, waiting for someone to come out and see what the noise was. We moved forward. Don laughed. Should have gone in and asked them for a push.

What were you doing before? I asked him. Well he said, I was good at drawing at school. I used to like that. Even got an art scholarship to the Poly. But it was a dead waste of time. Copy this, copy that. I just used to go on the roof and draw. So they kicked me out. Then I worked for a firm of sign writers. After that for Connors, the removal people, you know. And that old man Connor was really all right. You know the first time I went on the trot and they nicked me he came all the way down to Maidstone to see the C.O. and put in a good word for me. Said he'd never found anything wrong with my work and that my job was always open. Right decent bloke and I'd always thought he was a bit of an idiot. Nearly 3 a.m. We parked the van and went to sleep in the cab. We got about a fiver each for all the rubbish we'd nicked. But we did better afterwards.

~

In the dark I can't tell what the sandwiches are. Can't tell if the bread is white, or brown. The filling is meat. I'm sure of that. But it could be lamb, beef, or even chicken. And that worries me more than the dark and silence. And the liquid I drink is, I think, soup. But it could be onion, chicken, any variety of thin soup. So my sense of smell is affected. Each time I wake I check every part of my body by touch. The fingers, then up each arm to the shoulder, down my chest, my back, genitals, legs, feet, each toe. I leave my head to last. That's the strangest part, pressing my hands to my skull; feeling the limits of my shape while my mind is everywhere. I am a butterfly dreaming I am a man dreaming I am here.

Now Rinkoff is not true. He was the hero of an endless book I began to write in 1957 with Nigel Black. We were working for a company of pharmaceutical manufacturers and would type out a chapter a day on memo paper, sending them to each other through the internal mail system. Now only a few pages remain. Rinkoff the Demon Welder for example. Which reads like Nigel.

'This is not to be the story of his life. I hope we are all capable of that. No, what I want to try to do is to illuminate, or rather bring into relief, the demon which many of his friends could barely perceive in Rinkoff. "There's a demon in him" they would say, and forget about it.

Take his nose, for instance — surely a sign, a flag to fill one's eyes with apprehension. Sitting beside him in the car as he drove carefully through the Yorkshire Dales on their annual driving holiday, his wife glimpsed his nose in profile against the grey sky of late spring. She begged him to slow down. He merely remarked that when it started to rain, then he would slow down.

His eyes too; people had shied away from them as from a sudden wasp when he glanced at them from beneath his peaked cap and the shower of sparks flickered abruptly out.

Kosolapoff, who was his greatest friend in those days — youth I mean — was a man given to mischief. He was the greatest nuisance to shop stewards and management alike; he regarded them as mud on his boots. But he was always very meek when together with Rinkoff. Still, he was not dumb, Kosolapoff. He liked Rinkoff but he would never work alongside him. He always suspected the motives of those who had placed themselves in authority.

Of his early girl friends, only Petrella, the one without any breasts and hair down to her backside, suspected the demon in Rinkoff. It tickled her fancy, she said, to think of his picking up his arc lamp thing at night and stealing from bed to bed welding together the legs of all the virgins and spinsters in town. She was 28. She did not regard herself as a virgin or a spinster, but as a free woman. She hated cats.

One day they entered a coffee bar in Brighton, she in her suède jacket and yellow trousers, he in his black leather jacket and overalls, and got into a fight with the local intellectuals. It seemed to start because one of the bright-faced young girls turned her dove-eyes on Petrella and remarked to everyone that trousers, especially yellow trousers . . . '

And that's where it ends. There is one other piece. Which must be mine. At least it was printed under my name in a magazine called 'Thistle' in '59 or '60.

'11.30 p.m. Rinkoff typing. Stimulants: coffee, two thinly-rolled cigarettes. He types—

"Immense snowflakes fell that Sunday. They fell softly, gathering speed, finally hurtling down to crush with a soft thud the men who hid in the cracks of the paving-stones. And to hide their screams, the midday records, each dedicated like a wreath, played louder . . ."

Rinkoff paused. It wasn't *exactly* what he had wanted to say. He pulled the paper from the machine and wrote in pencil "Imagine slightly to the left of this paragraph". Winding in a new sheet he began again—

"Would the men be crushed, or would the snow, jam-like, cream-like, soft-squelch on their heads and trickle down, the result like a pegless tent? Would the tiger spread like toothpaste across the road? His tiger? Does snow harm tigers? Tigers eat snow and the result is a cold mouth." He drank some coffee and continued.

March. Rinkoff's first novel was published that month, consisting of the following sentences:

> Jason lived in a house
> Jason dwelt in a dwelling
> Jason existed in a den
> Jason lodged in a home
> Jason resided in a residence
> Jason stayed in a mansion

Each sentence was printed in the exact centre of a sheet of thick paper. These sheets could, by an ingenious system of spiral binding, be arranged in any order. The order gave the plot, Rinkoff said, and the plot gave the order. Most readers arranged the sheets like this:

> Jason lived in a house
> Jason resided in a residence
> Jason stayed in a mansion
> Jason lodged in a home
> Jason dwelt in a dwelling
> Jason existed in a den

as their minds had been well conditioned to the order of things. Rinkoff got a good laugh out of this.'

It was while working for the same company that I met Bert Swanwick, Bill, Arthur, Sid. Driving down to Dartford ('59) in the firm's van with Arthur, talking about Bill. Old

Bill's tin, he said. Oh yeh. He used to keep it in the back of his van. Stank like fuck it did. It was Len started it. Let's knock a hole in it he said. So I said Be a bit cunning. If you knock one big hole in the middle he's bound to notice. I got a very thin nail and knocked little tiny holes all round the bottom. He went to piss in it next day in the yard. Laugh! All over his shoes and trousers. Best thing was at first he never noticed it. And a bloody long piss it was. He was chatting away; never felt a thing. When he'd finished he shook the tin, you know, to shake it out on the ground. Don't know why he bothered; why he didn't just piss straight on the ground. But he'd always use his tin and then empty it out. Habit. So this time nothing came out. So you know what the stupid bleeder does? He looks inside. Must have thought it had stuck to the bottom like treacle. Then he saw his shoes. Christ! You should have heard him. But that bloody thing really used to stink. He kept it in the back of his van, see. And then if he wanted to go while he was driving he'd haul it out, piss, open the window and empty it. Pity anyone behind him on a motorbike. I reckon he's the filthiest bloke I know. I ever tell you about the day he shit hisself? No? Well, he comes in one morning looking a bit miserable, see. So I say What's up Bill? And he says Christ I've got the bloody shits this morning. Messed meself on the way in. What did you do? I say. Go back home? No he says, I won't be a minute, just going down to the bog. Brought a clean pair of pants with you? I ask him. He says No, these'll be all right, just turn'm inside out. And that's what he did. Didn't even bother to scrape it off I suppose. He didn't mind the smell, see, just the feel of it next to his skin. Filthy bastard. My old piss-can he called it. Got all furred-up one time, like a kettle. Look at this he tells me. Bit of boiling water ought to get that out Bill I said. But that wasn't good enough for him. Oh no. He had to fill it with Lysol or carbolic. Something like that. Burn the stuff away I suppose he thought. Bloody giggle though. He was late the next day. Turned out he'd forgotten he'd put in this stuff. On the way to work he'd started to piss and it'd splashed all over his cock. Burned like fuck he said. Had to smear ointment all over it. Nearly burned me bloody knob off he told me. And his trousers kept rubbing the sore patches. From what I can gather him and his old woman've got some place over a shop. Falling to pieces I hear. So he started to nick cardboard cartons from Packing. I watched him taking them for about a month, then one day I asked him about it. Seems one of his walls had fallen down, so he'd got these cartons, flattened them out and wired them together. Then he'd fixed up the hole with them. Even covered them with plaster and paint. You ask Bert. He went round there one day when Bill was off sick to take him his money. Bill was laying there, heaving and panting like a porpoise and Bert was chatting to him. Nowhere to sit, so he goes to lean on the wall. Get off there you nutter says Bill. You'll go right through. Sure enough Bert feels this wall and it was all them cardboard boxes. Swayed backwards and forwards. That place must be falling apart. And his old woman. He comes in one morning. The old woman was bad last night he says. Up all bloody night with her I was. Every time I dozed off she was groaning and twitching. Pains in her back or something. So I says Up a minute you silly bitch. No wonder you've got a pain, your bloody arse is hanging on the floor. The frame of the bed had gone, see, and the mattress was sagging through the hole. So he goes down to his yard and pulls out a couple of scaffold boards. Takes them back upstairs. Lift your arse a minute he says. Then he sticks these boards between the frame and the mattress to sort of keep it level like. So in the end she got some sleep. When he told me about this I said Well, didn't the boards stick out a bit? Yes he says, but they thought it was a good idea. Said his old woman could put her tea on it. Sort of like a bedside table. But then she got really ill. Woke him again one night. Said she felt sick and wanted to piss as well. Make up your mind you silly cow he said. What do you want to do first? She was in such a state she didn't know. So he picks up his can. Holds it under her chin. But he'd guessed wrong, and while he's holding it there she pissed all over the floor. But what can you do with him? He came down the canteen this afternoon, after he'd been messing around with his motor. Grease all over his hands. So he comes downstairs and the woman from the canteen has given us a big can of left-over chips. He reaches in, grabs a hand-ful and stuffs'm in his mouth. I say What, diesel oil as well Bill? And he mutters something about A bit of dirt never hurt no-one.

Or Sid the chauffeur a year later. Sitting in the office wait-ing for the manager to sign some petrol chits. You know, he said, I'd rather earn it than spend it. I hate spending money. I'd rather scrub out a room than go shopping. I used to work for a millionaire, he went on, a long while ago. Before the war that was. He had this daughter died of a malignant growth. Had a steam-yacht. Been all round the world. He'd served his time as a mining engineer in Russia. Rolling in it he was. I'd have liked some of it, not a lot, just enough to be comfortable. You know, they were so bloody victorian that this girl wouldn't take her knickers off, even to have a bath. Not even if her mother was there with her. They must have spent thousands on her during the years I was there. One time they had this doctor up from London. I had to pick him up and drive him out. He looked at her for about five minutes, had an enormous dinner with her old man, then I had to drive him back. That's all he did. Next day he sent in a bill for a hundred guineas. Must have sat up that same night and wrote it out. Dietician he was. The butler said to me Here, that bloke you brought out was a right one wasn't he? Why? I say. He said Well, he sent in a bill for a hundred guineas this morning. And he went into the office and fetched it out for me to see. Didn't spend more than five minutes with her. Then there was this other doctor from Bond Street. He was too busy to come himself so he sent an assistant. Came out four times, gave her four injections: two hundred quid. She died of course. About half an hour after she went the old lady came to see me. Could you come upstairs and take the fittings down quietly? she asked. I went up to the bathroom and there were pulleys and ropes and god knows what. So she could pull herself up from her chair and into the bath. I started to take them

[56]

down and dropped a pulley. The old lady came in to see what was wrong. Would you like to see Miss May? she asked me. Well, I went into her room. She'd been dead only half an hour and they already had this artist chap in there. She'd had lovely long black hair and he'd spread it over the pillow like a fan. He'd crossed her arms and put a bunch of flowers on her chest and was sketching her like that. You know I could have kissed that girl she looked so lovely. They cut down one of the elm trees on the estate to make her coffin. And she was driven all through the village. Me and the other chauffeur were up on the roof taking photographs. Then they turned up the drive to this old ruined chapel that was in the grounds. And you know what? They had a bishop down to consecrate a patch of ground behind this chapel so she could be buried there. And for a week the whole family ate every meal beside her grave. Every meal! The butler had to bring them out on trays. Lovely girl she was. I had a silver cigarette case in her will. Actually I had the choice of that, or an ashtray. Her mother wrote a history of her. I was mentioned in it in connection with the amateur dramatics we used to have. Before she got really bad I used to take her to parties and things in London. One night I was sick and they had to hire a car. You know they sat up all night till she got in. Butler and all. These young undergraduates used to escort her home. And when I'd taken her in they'd say I've got to get back to town you know. And I'd say Well, you better call a taxi. Can you lend me ten bob then? they'd say. And I'd have to take them because I knew I'd never see the money again. That history was all printed up in a big book. About a foot square. With that artist's picture of her in the front. You couldn't buy it of course. But I've still got a copy at home.

The spy-school was fascinating and I forgot Louise. Forgot her that is until the photograph was burning in front of me. And then I remembered everything. The room was square. A wooden table. Four wooden chairs with curved plywood backs. The floor of thin wooden boards, not polished. A round glass ashtray on the table. A glass dish. The window in the middle of the wall opposite the door. Lace curtains with flower patterns. Three rows of bookshelves each side of the window. And under the left-hand bookshelves another shelf. On it a sugar bowl with a silver top, two twisted red candles, a green glass jug. The walls beige, the ceiling white. In the right-hand corner a three-drawer chest. On it an alarm clock, a radio, a lamp with no shade and a small bear with a gold chain round its neck. The bed upholstered in orange. A wardrobe with two cases on the top; one black, bound with brass, the other fawn. Beside it a picture, and under the picture, on the floor, a record player with a grey fan-heater next to it. What colour are the walls of *this* room? In this darkness would it make any difference if they were white? Nothing to reflect. The one flaw in my mechanism is that I cannot switch myself off.

Oh it was interesting. Codes and cyphers. Weapons and exercises. That was before the improvements. I made friends with a deaf mute. He'd been born over there;

spoke their language. Not spoke of course. What I mean is his language was theirs. So now his job was to watch every piece of film we got from them, of their parades, their public meetings, and lip-read. To decipher what those in the background were saying. But they must have known we had men like him. And planted their own in the crowds to clearly enunciate false trails. He defected one day. Perhaps he saw his name spoken by a scruffy man behind a cordon of police. Perhaps an offer was made to him in a General's aside to his Aide. Or someone he had loved brought from miles away to stand in the crowd at a fashion show. A weakness I no longer have. Then it was passion, tenderness and love. Distortions of direction. Now my perspective is true. And for the women the act is better. My electronic organ extending, changing length and width and shape, holding for as long as they want. Would she love me now, Louise?

Alf I'd known from grammar-school. Black hair and brown eyes. Exchanging science-fiction books was what brought us together. We tried to convert our English master whose major achievement was a thirty-page booklet on the life of some obscure African saint. No, not even a saint then, just Blessed something. We never succeeded with him, but we did with a few of the others in the class. I've always had a good memory for books I lend to people. Kevin Considine has my copy of *Expedition to Earth* that he borrowed the week before I left school. Not that I want it back now; that's just the way my mind works. As I always know the balance between cigarettes I give to people and those they offer back. And other things. Like how many different coloured Smarties there are. I can tell you that now: eight. And I can name them: dark brown, light brown, purple, pink, red, green, yellow and orange. And forty-three or sometimes forty-four in each of those little tubes.

They sat there in that orderly room. Straight lines, the fireplace really in the wrong wall, and played the game. Talking. Did you see that film? she asked, Light in the Piazza? Isn't that some sort of Italian pie? he asked. No she said, that's Pisa. I thought that was a French toilet he came back. Oh, a patisserie she said. And the other woman suddenly woke up and said Isn't that a French cake shop? They stopped and stared at her.

The bottle fell to the floor. She picked it up and dipped the teat in the water. Why don't you wash the fucking thing? he said to her. She said But I rinsed it. Yes he shouted, the fucking TIP I suppose you think germs can't JUMP.

It became impossible for him to stop playing the game. You're not normal she told him. I've never been a garage. The visitors looked at him puzzled. And how could he explain to them the chain: normal norman norman norman mailer norman mailer the deer park deer park dear park dear expensive a dear park park a car park a dear car park a garidge at claridges claridges' garage.

The greengrocer said I don't think it's fair on your wife

to have it more than once a week if she's working. See,
I've got a little bird up Highbury, Shirl her name is. She's
got a nice little place so I shoot up there.

That Brian, don't know what's the matter with him said
Joan. You know he wanted it guess how many ... THREE
TIMES last week. I'm bleedin worn out. It was Joan who
had said to his wife when she went to borrow a colander
to drain some spaghetti Oh, you don't have to throw that
tomato sauce away you know, you can eat it. And again,
watching his wife cooking, Oh, I see, you *cheat*. Meaning
she was using a recipe.

Jimmy I met in the west end. He'd been drifting around
there for years. Had just got a job in a shop selling porno-
graphic books, films and photographs. He was only the
front man; the job lasted until the shop was raided. The
average time between raids was four months, but a friend
of his had lasted seven. Of course the shop never closed;
just changed the name and manager. He said it was interesting for the first couple of days. Odd people coming in,
and looking through the stock himself. But after that it
was a drag, sitting there six days a week. But the money
was good. £5 a day cash, no tax, no insurance stamp, no
deductions. So he was making £30 a week clear. The day
he was arrested he would get £50 and the £5 daily would
continue until his trial. The owners of course paid all
costs, fines and so on. If he was sent to jail, £5 a day would
be paid into an account for him while he was inside. And
there was even a bonus system. £20 extra a week if the

shop's takings exceeded £100 a day . . . and he got that bonus every week he was there. I'll tell you something he said to me. I'll tell you what the best-selling photograph is this week. It's a bird dressed in a frogman's suit, all you can see is her eyes, and she's tied to this kitchen chair with a piece of rope. All the old boys are going nutty over it. Can't understand it. I mean what can they get out of that?

~

In which country am I? I have no idea. Yes my defenses are functioning perfectly. The latest memories being erased. At least, erased in so far as I cannot recall them. But inside me they are perfectly recorded. On a level to which I have no access. No cover for them to crack. I don't even know who they are; who the enemy is. Each time they question me I lie and invent. Whatever they finally decide to believe, that is the truth. A covering of insanity I can finally pull around me. Louise. No. I'd left Louise. It was Don I was thinking about. He showed me some of his paintings once. Not very good. A little better than choco-late-box. And his series of drawings of William Bendix. He loved westerns and we'd go to all the old ones repeated for one day only on Sundays. Three years after I last saw him I heard he'd married Jackie. And their first kid was a boy. Shane Clint Brett he called him.

When I'm rich he said, you know what I'm going to do? Open a club. That's what I fancy. Drink, a lot of birds, a bit of gambling, music. We were walking down the High Street. A Wednesday. Early closing day. How much you got on you? he asked. About three quid I told him. Well listen he said, you got anything on this evening? No, I was just going to have a few drinks I told him, and get an early night. He went on You know Brown's, where Jackie's been working? I nodded. Well, they have a load of scrap to shift every few weeks. And they got no yard to store it see, so they load up a truck in the afternoon, park it outside all night and move it the next morning. It'll be down there tonight. You game? We can get a good price at Dave's.

Good bit of lead in there, some brass, all that sort of stuff.
O.K. I said, come round for me about nine.

From the hill the road sloped down and to the right. A
dark grey bird with an orange beak skimmed across,
paused on a wooden fence, shat, then continued its curve
as the blob fell. All the way on the tube he kept thinking
of the line 'And we walk through the valley of the fables
where the eagles lie.' It was going to rain. The colours of
the flowers hurt his eyes.

He stood in a doorway watching the place where he'd
arranged to meet her. One of his habits. Like conspicu-
ously checking his watch when security men delivered
money. Like always looking round furtively when getting
into a car. She got off the bus. Peered at her reflection in
a shop window and patted her hair. He walked over.

Before leaving his room he had arranged everything. Left
the bed made, the curtains pulled. Sorted out the records.
Put two glasses by the whiskey bottle. He hid the telephone in a drawer in case she checked the number.
Washed and shaved. Put on a shirt, jeans, a jacket. No
underwear.

She was wearing a yellow linen costume. A black and
white spotted silk blouse. And began to talk immediately.
Her English was good, certain German phrasings, but the
pitch was too high. Not a pleasant voice to listen to. I have
been reading this book by a Christopher Isherwood? she

told him. Good Bye to Ber Lin. Do you know of it? I quite like it; it is how I feel. Christ he thought and stopped listening. 'We walk through the valley of fables' or 'the valley of *the* fables'? Where are we going? she asked. I have free until eleven.

When they got off the train he took her by a complicated route. Approached the house from the back. They went in and she looked at the room. Stood in the middle and stared at everything. Sit down he said. And put on a record. Slow organ music. Gave her a cigarette. Yes she said, I quite like it here, it is nice. He poured himself a drink. Offered her one. She refused. Look she continued, I have this letter from France offering me a job. Only two children to look after and teach the eldest one English. I prefer that, you know, to teach English. Those other families want me for German lessons but how? It is my language but I could not teach, I do not know the rules. But English I have learned properly. Yes he said to her and pulled her up to dance. Slowly. He kissed her. She danced heavily, no balance, a weight to push. Then they stopped moving their feet; just swayed. He kissed her again, holding the back of her neck with his right hand, rubbing his left across her breasts, over the silk. At the end of the track he left her standing and finished his drink. I think I have one now she told him. He half-filled a glass with whiskey, poured in some ginger ale, and gave it to her. Then started to take off her jacket. Oh stop she said and they danced some more. It was already dark outside. And raining. The only light in the room a reflection from the street lamps; a red glow from the bulb on the record player. He undid the buttons at the back of her blouse. Moved his hands inside and scratched her back; she leaned against him. His prick was hard against her thigh; he nudged her with it. The record finished. Putting the needle back to the beginning he sat on the bed, pulled her down on his knee. She was talking again. He listened for a moment . . . This French boy I went out with, it is always the same, one evening he said to me now I have two questions to ask you. The first is will you stay with me tonight? I said No. Then he said My second question is what then is the purpose of our relationship? Sharp, he thought, and undid her brassiere. Slipped her blouse forward and released her breasts. She stopped talking and leaned back. He rested on his left elbow, kissing her, pulling her nipple with his finger and thumb. Stroked her shoulder with his nose. Slid his tongue under her arm. Then licked her breasts, first one, then the other. He put her hand between his legs and she squeezed. Still kissing her he pushed his hand under her skirt and stroked her leg gently, just above the top of her stocking. She kept her eyes closed, but pressed her thighs together. He pushed his knee between her legs from underneath. Took his hand away and felt for the zip of her skirt. It was at the back. She was still holding him, not moving her hand, just squeezing. He sucked at her breast; hairs round the nipple. Pulled one out with his teeth. She jerked and opened her eyes. Wait she said. He went to change the record and she stood up. Like a picture from any pin-up magazine: a standard pose. One leg slightly forward, one shoulder down, her breasts bare, undoing her suspenders. Then she lay back on the bed. He sat beside her, pushing her legs apart with his hand. She felt for him again, and he undid the zip to let her hand inside. Took off his shirt while her hand was moving. Your trousers as well, she told him. Then put her arms behind his head and pulled him down, his hand trapped between them. He rubbed the side of his finger against her cunt. Oh no she said but still held his head tightly to her. Oh no. Moving a little now as he pressed against her. Oh no and her thighs relaxed a little. Then Ah, that is *nice*, but no more, it is too dangerous. He had two fingers inside her now. She moved her head sideways on the pillow and he licked inside her ear. Took her hand from his neck and pulled it down between them. She moved it back when it touched him. Come on he said, that's all it is. What are you frightened of? Oh no she said. He kissed her to shut out that voice, feeling her teeth with his tongue, pushing it into her mouth until she was sucking it, moving, rolling his prick against her leg. Turning on to his side he looked at her, one hand still between her legs. There were teeth-marks on her shoulder and she opened her eyes and smiled at him. Streaks of eye make-up on the pillow. He took both her hands and held them. Kiss me again she said and he bent forward. His tongue in her navel, chin pressing into her belly, one hand on her breast the other back between her legs. Then moved them both to her knees, and parting them, pushed down his head. Oh she said, no, what are you doing? No, she said, it is not ... But his tongue was probing and she groaned as his teeth

[67]

nipped her gently. One of his hands was underneath her now, pressing her to his face, the fingers wet. Then, his tongue still working, he pushed a finger into the other hole. She tensed, then moved faster, backwards and forwards, side to side. Ohhhh please . . . he heard her . . . what . . . ahhhhhhhh . . . that is *nice*. Again. She shuddered and relaxed. He lay down beside her again, prick sore where she had clutched it. She cuddled against him and pulled a blanket over them. Mmmmmmmmmmm, feeling him still hard. Got out of bed, poured two drinks and brought him one. He sat up, pushing back the blanket. She leaned against him. What is the time? Nine, he told her. And at ten I must go she said. My lady does not like it for me to be late. Taking his glass, she put it with hers on the floor under the bed.

Lay on her stomach looking at him. He patted her behind. Faint line of hair along the spine. It was good that I met you she said. I can talk to you. With most English people it is so difficult. Hug me now? she asked him, I feel cold. Scratching his balls with one finger. In a minute he told her. I have to go outside. She asked him Why? To piss. Oh she said, I have never seen a man doing it. Can I come with you? Do what you like he said, irritated. He didn't want to talk to her but still wanted to screw her. When they were standing she kissed him, both hands on his shoulders. He opened the door and they went down the corridor to the bathroom. Don't you have any brothers? he asked her. She answered Yes, but they are only small. It is funny, she went on, that you have to stand. And sat on the edge of the bath. Can I hold it? she said, while you're doing it? His prick was hard again and her hands were cold. He had to bend forward so it went into the pan. She still held him when he'd finished, leaning forward looking at it. Pushing it against her he took her breasts in both hands and squeezed them round it. Her nipples hardened against his stomach. But it is so cold in here she said, suddenly getting up. Let us go back in the other room. Looking at himself in the mirror he followed her. She was hiding behind the door; caught him from behind as he walked in. Hands around his waist kissing the back of his neck. He pushed back, feeling her hairs rub his buttocks. Put the fire on he told her, taking the pillows from the bed and putting them on the floor. Adding the cushions from the two chairs. As she bent to plug in the fire he pushed against her from behind. No she said, we must not. It is too dangerous. He pulled her on to the floor, tongue going into her mouth. To stop that voice. She wriggled underneath him, pulling, squeezing. He realised what she was trying to do: to make him come now. And taking her hands away he pushed them underneath, so the weight of her body kept them there. Boredom was winning. Her eyes were closed again. She was saying something in German. He caught the word *verführt*. Pushed himself slowly into her. Again she was saying No . . . no . . . but her legs tightened around him. Then he pulled himself free and got up. Switched on the TV and put on his jeans. She watched him. But I do not understand you . . . she shook her head. Come ON he told her. What do you take me for? You want it both ways, don't you? You want me to fuck you and all the time you're saying NO NO NO. So you can have the pleasure and still feel I've forced you to do it. You stupid bitch you're unHEALTHY. So why should I give you that satisfaction? seDUCE you he went on. What the hell do you see yourself as? Either you want to fuck or you don't. If you don't, that's straight enough. It's your privilege. But if you do, you got to give a little bit more than the ACTION. God it's a wonder you didn't start by telling me I wouldn't resPECT you. You're dumb enough to believe that. Come on he said as she dressed, it's nearly ten, you better go. He put on his shirt and jacket and went out with her. She didn't speak. When they got to the High Street he pointed. The station's down there, he told her. I got to go back now, there's something I want to watch. What will you do? she asked him. Will you telephone to me? O.K. he said and turned back. It began to rain again. When he got in he dried his hair. Sat by the fire. He didn't want to drink. There was half a joint in a drawer. He turned on and watched the TV till it shut down. Stayed watching the screen after the National Anthem until the voice said Don't forget to switch off your set, will you. Then he went to sleep.

Don came round for me at nine. November. Already dark, a cold wind blowing straight down the street. Offered me a cigarette. We stopped to light up. Then walked towards the railway bridge. You know, I told him, we had a great party here after the war. The week after V.J. day I think. In fact every street had one. Tables down the middle of the road. All the kids. Some I'd never seen before. Back from being evacuated. I even got to go to two because we lived on the corner. First our street, then this one. We had sandwiches, lemonade, paper hats. Somebody's mum had even got a hold of a couple of those gallon drums of ice-cream from somewhere. First I ever tasted. I got back after all that, Don said. I was evacuated up the Lake District. Pissing horrible. They really used to hate us, those yokels. I'd rather have been here getting bombed. Crossing the bridge. I remember before they built this, I told him. Used to be a level crossing here. I remember being wheeled here in my pram. Waiting for the gates to open. Shall we call for Joe? I asked him. No he said, he gets on my nerves lately. Flash bastard. And soft as shit underneath. If the law got hold of him he'd shop you as soon as they coughed. He lit another cigarette. And said Let's have a drink before we go. We went into a pub opposite the park gates. I saw Frankie Peters he went on, this afternoon. Just after you went home. He got out of the kate all right. Reckoned his old man bunged someone a hundred quid. But I don't quite credit that somehow. Probably got perforated eardrums, or flat feet. Or maybe he's colour-blind I said. He laughed. Very funny. You remember Frankie up the drill-hall that night? I asked. The time he went off with the Gobbler? Christ, she was a real mess wasn't she? Looked like she never washed. And Frankie's pissed as a newt, isn't he. Has a couple of dances with her, then they're away outside into the bushes. Half an hour later he's back. Comes over. All right? I ask him. Cause he was dead unlucky every time he pulled a bird. Nothin' there, was there, he'd say. But this time he's really chuffed. I take her out the back, he tells me, and we're having a bit of a lumber. I've got her tits out and she's having a feel. So I ask her What about it then? And she says All right. So I've got me flies open, her skirt's up, she's got no pants on. I have a quick bit of finger and then I try to get it in. We're up against this tree, see. Can't get down on the ground cause it's been raining. Puffing and panting away but I can't get nowhere. Too awkward. Can't you do something? I say to her. And all of a sudden she's squatting down there plating me. Mouth straight on to it. I'm so surprised I've come before I know what's happened. Then she stands up. O.K.? she says, and starts combing her hair. Yeh, Don said laughing, nobody ever called her nothing but the Gobbler after that. Can't even remember what her real name is. Shall we make a move? I finished my drink and we left.

We caught a trolley-bus. Got off at the Clock Tower and walked through the back streets to Brown's. A truck was parked outside. Quiet. No-one about. Keep an eye out while I get it started Don said. When the engine was running I got in. We drove towards the arterial road. I had a word with Dave on the blower said Don, he'll be waiting for us. A bell began to ring somewhere. In the mirror I saw a black Wolseley behind us. It's the law Don, I said. Well he asked, what do you want to do? I said, We're not going to race that motor of theirs in this thing, that's sure. Whatever we do they're going to nick us. So we just pull up easy, no bother. We just took this on impulse, didn't we? Just for a drive about. We were going to put it back, and we got no idea what's in the back. Right? Don nodded.

Slowed down and pulled in to the kerb. The law stopped in front of us and one of them got out. Oh shit Don said, it's Clark. He knows me. We were at school together. Snydy git. Just stick to what I said I told him. Clark opened the door of the cab. All right lads he said, outside. We've got a few little questions to ask you. This lorry's been reported as stolen. Already? I said, we've only been in it five minutes. We have our sources he told me. Even before they coughed, I said to Don. He nodded. We climbed down. Clark grinned when he saw Don. Well well well he said, *isn't* that nice. My old friend. We've had a little letter about *you* from the Army. They'll be pleased to see *you* again. Just doing a bit of thieving to pass the time? Thieving what? I asked him. We only took this for a drive around. Who's your friend? he asked Don, nodding at me. I don't think we've met before. You must introduce me. Come on he continued, into the car. We got in the back. Clark sat next to the driver and we moved off. What happens if someone nicks that lorry now? I said. Oh said the driver, you *are* a little comedian, *aren't* you.

They drove us straight to Bexleyheath police station. Into the yard, through the door at the back, and up the stairs into the C.I.D. room. Now said the sergeant there, empty your pockets on to this table. We'll give you a nice tidy receipt for everything. Then we're going to lock you up for a little while. I'll be making a little call to the M.P.'s about *you*: he flicked his thumb at Don. And then after that we'll have a nice cosy chat with you both. But one at a time. He took us downstairs and locked us in separate cells. I looked around. High ceiling. Small barred window at the top of the wall opposite the door. Concrete floor. Walls and ceiling painted with Government Office Cream Gloss. A thick water pipe running under the window. On the right, a low bunk covered with a grey blanket. At the end of that an open toilet. I sat on the bed for a few minutes. Then got up and walked about. Nearly the whole surface of the door was covered with scratched messages. I didn't bother to read them. Carefully I went through my pockets, pulling out the linings. In the top one of my jacket I found a plastic tooth broken from a comb. I began to scratch my initials and the date. Brown varnish flaking off as I picked away. About half an hour afterwards I heard them come for Don. Then it was quiet again. I felt nervous, but not afraid. Interested in what was happening. I'm still there.

∾

Noon. Jerome on his way to the Studios. Nervously buying an extra packet of cigarettes to avoid changing a pound note on the bus. French cigarettes, but tipped. His hair sticking up on one side where he'd slept on it. Feeling the day like a thin plate in front of him.

The bus stop had been moved, though several people were standing beside the blank pole. Some drunk had thrown the temporary sign into a front garden during the night. Jerome stood by the kerb, alone. The unofficial queue stared at him. As it began to rain, he lit a cigarette. A removal van pulled up beside the old stop and two men began to unload furniture on to the pavement. A chest of drawers (walnut veneer): a motorcycle: two grand pianos. The queue were engrossed, huddling against the side of the van to avoid the rain. At high speed the bus passed them, stopped briefly beside Jerome and sped off. The conductor grinned.

Jerome on the top deck, back seat. Whistling 'Now's the Time' to show the cool conductor he knows. Click click Conductor X I'm with YOU. The immigrant smiling as he takes Jerome's money—Now what's THAT you're smoking? Jerome answering Actually it's a FRENCH cigarette. Offering the packet. A match. The conductor, stamping his foot three times to speed the driver past a request stop saying Hmmmmmm . . . not bad. A pause. Jerome trying to fill it . . . I brought them back with me . . . I go over there quite a lot . . . in fact I'm going next week . . . maybe I could send you a couple of packets. Running off two feet

[75]

of blank ticket paper the conductor writing his address: Osman Lincoln Mannerman, 15 Harthorn Road, Islington, London N.7. Jerome on the platform saying to him Great. Looking at the strip of paper. On the end in violet ink NOT TRANSFERABLE.

As he landed on the pavement, running, he collided with an old woman. Bowed politely, said Excuse me, smiled. She looked past him and shoved her wheeled shopping basket between his legs. Going into a doorway out of the rain Jerome took a card from his wallet, sealed it in an envelope and ran after her. Tapped her on the shoulder —I believe you dropped this. Crossed the road as she was opening it. On the deckle-edged card, in small heavy gothic type GOD THINKS YOU'RE UGLY. A car stopped beside him and he misdirected the driver to avoid embarrassment.

What should be told about Jerome is that the part that could be seen was nothing. Imogen had given him her love and three fast children. The oldest child, Dorcas, had the most beautiful verbs. Scissor me a piece of paper she would say, or, Oven the bread NOW. One Sunday morning she had broken into Jerome's dream to open the window and shout Daddy Daddy . . . there's a man lawning the grass. Then Jerome had known that it was spring and she was surely destined to die of a lingering painful disease that even curare couldn't cure. But he had shouted at her WHY don't you stay in your fucking room out of the WAY! Inside him was a kind and courteous man, Jerome knew, but that had ceased to give him satisfaction. Travelling away from home the sight of a small child would knot his stomach. Tonight, he told himself, I will bow gently to them all and expose the part of me that is real. I am a nice man, he thought, to be on the edge of. But anyone closer gets burned in the oven.

Imogen paid the milkman and made the bed. Without thinking she tidied Jerome's papers, sliding today's letters under last week's, tapping the edges square. She set his typewriter to 'stencil' and left a box full of dead matches beside it. Taking his last envelope with her, she moved the picture above his desk slightly askew and went into the kitchen. He had left a Penguin face downwards on the grill-pan. One paragraph was marked. 'Presently all objects enter into their own shadows, and through the general veil then formed the stars become apparent.' You're putting me on she thought. And went shopping.

Jerome entering the Studios. Saying Fly Jefferson Airplane to the commissionaire. Into his office. To his secretary Good morning Miss Brown. Here's half a crown. Get'm down. Drowning her reply with But SERIOUSLY Coral you've the MOST BEAUTIFULLY DEVELOPED xerasia of any girl in this company. (softly) Suck my Dick. (louder) I said Send for Dick. Please. He unlocked his desk and shot a grain of heroin for his bronchitis.

Wednesday May 22nd. And I have bronchitis. 7 p.m. It's been a hot, dry day in Granada. Chris brought me a half bottle of anis. I tried to make a transfer charge call to England but it was refused. So what happened to Jerome and Imogen? To Rinkoff, Don, Alf and Jimmy? To the re-made agent? To Gerry in his hotel room? To Louise and the German au-pair? Are you interested? That's the plot. And the form is the title. Or think about this:

Lloyd: What's B.O.? Val: Smell from sweat. Lloyd: So why don't they say Freedom from smelly sweat then? Why B.O. so children don't understand?

What happened to the life we were going to probe and investigate? I'm just going to sit here staring at the Sierra Nevada, listening to the trains going in and out of the station. Watching the mountains change shape as the sun moves. In two hours' time I'll have another injection. Maybe a piece of the bread and cheese Roy brought me. Or a glass of the Campari we stole from a hotel in Almuñécar. The swallows are circling and the taxis are gathering underneath my window. And when I can answer Ben's last two questions I'll know what to do. The questions?

> What's brown's second colour?
> What's mauve together?

That's what I meant all the time he said.

LETTERS FROM YADDO

The hammer-cloth happened to be unusually gorgeous; and partly on that consideration, but partly also because the box offered the most elevated seat, was nearest to the moon, and undeniably went foremost, it was resolved by acclamation that the box was the imperial throne, and for the scoundrel who drove, he might sit where he could find a perch.

— 'The English Mail-Coach' (THOMAS DE QUINCEY)

Dear Ed:

Sorry to have missed you when I called, but I was happy to hear Jenny and to learn that you are all o.k. I got here yesterday on the bus from New York: now it's a bright spring morning. I think I'll keep some kind of journal . . . no . . . what I mean is I'll type out the past day's events each morning and mail it to you. That way I won't have a copy to read with hindsight. I feel nervous about carbons—they're really secretive. So what's new? I had a card from Anselm waiting for me saying there's nothing in Iowa (which I'd known for about 33 years) and that he has doubts about his job. Before I left Colchester I wrote a joke poem which, on re-reading, seems to say all I can about England:—

Sonnet Daze

i watch myself grow larger in her eyes
and clutch a yellow feather near its tip
as if to mark with ink that never dries
the yet uncharted voyage of my ship

those two flat images project and form
the looming solid that contains my mind
whilst independently the quill writes "warm"
dreaming its tip still in the bird's behind

since those two stanzas many days have passed
now percy thrower speaks of roses on t.v.
morecambe and wise with full supporting cast
will soon be on—i call for val to see

the fire is red   the cat licks down her tail
i close my eyes and read the rest in braille

What else? Yes, Val and the children came out to the airport with me (shit . . . why don't I just write a book and send it? . . . I mean what was I thinking of . . . a journal . . . jesus, I can see it bound in leather with JOURNAL stamped on the cover). O.K. We're in the book. So easy. Like being alive. I can't stop laughing. Right. Val and the children came out to the airport with me, then went down to her mother's, on the coast, for a few days. That 'flu hung around a long time, and Val got it last, so I hope the sea air blows it away. Jenny said you were going into the country. Will you be in Chicago around May 16th/17th? I have to leave on the 18th in the afternoon.

I got worried about writing the other day. Sitting talking to someone—or, rather, listening to someone talk—I caught myself making mental notes of what was being said to write up later. Not only that, but I got really irritated with the person talking because I was having to file the memory rapidly at the back of my head so I could listen to the radio to catch the name of a record that was playing and the voice was drowning it out. So I scribbled it all down as it was, because I realised that's what a writer is, and you can only use yourself in the most truthful way possible at the time (by the way, this book is called AMERICA LEAVES). This is what I wrote:—

> not writing the truth. writing that. holding that in my head while i bitch to myself about the dialogue because i can't hear the name of the record. thanks, jack: although your death is as sadness in aspic in ted's poem. buying your time and space and thinking about it. the forks are character and life. take life. from the intersection a silver bus shimmers towards me in the heat haze. a blue shape crosses the road. now you'd be interested if this were a

character, re-appearing from the separation of character and life. jimi hendrix castles made of sand. if this is not true it wouldn't work and how would you know? pause about your head. skyline i'm interested in. i mean the machine has limits . . . not only the people you 'happen to run into', but the basketball game. bradley and barnett. don't look . . . don't look at him. car horn from outside, crumpled paper from within. the breeze rustles the leaves of the sweet potato plant. all grit is left in the grille. so i'm not going to sublimate it by putting it into the mouths of 'characters' . . . or/and letting them take over. if you can't give it straight, there's no point in being a radio (radio-lib stand up!) this is a trip through the world of writing, vicarious heads. if you want to work *that* slowly, here comes the cancer. and i don't want a piece of YOU to mature in my pouch now that tape is running through me. you know . . . they filter it off into interviews while 'we want food' comes through in blurred waves. so let's give them content that extends to any flat edge they'd call 'form'. i scream it out through this maze of pines. i love you (all of you i love, that is). keep everyone in the world awake at the same time (synchronized alarm clocks) and we all disappear.

Now I'm sure I had a note from a couple of days ago that ties in with that. My yellow pencil shakes with the vibration of the typewriter and I stop to read its inscription: THINK AND SUGGEST — STATE OF N.J.500. My notebook now. No. Looks like I never wrote it down. But here's all that's there: —

APRIL 1ST

> very profound
> and almost round
>
> the story of the three verbs
> light   time   and space
>
> their coast
> isn't my coast

~

> good evening
> i am worn away by your kisses
> god i was good

~

> that song
> that you remember

~

turning and turning and turning it is really scandalous
how we jump up and down on the international date
line. i follow the sun — and they call them the back-
ward nations

~

another pretentious english group
thinking the audience is a mirror

∼

on the streets again
doing my confidence trick, trock

∼

a message from the stars in cancer through radio
waves. oscar wilde/fingal's cave. tulips took over the
dutch economy. every picture tells a story. i think,
therefore thought is. descartes'/leonardo's whirlpools.
recreate the past. we are the product of people's battles
inside our heads. it has been the presence, or personality, of artists . . . not their work. or why the academies
don't like 'anecdotal'.

∼

APRIL 8

PICTURES e.g. ed amd me in cambridge. neil rennie,
hugo and me at lunch. packet of 10 embassy. 2 gold leaf
packets. '29' on building opposite. chenille lions on
wall. hugo's discoloured tooth (right hand side). flakes
of (the bill was £1.97) rice (yellow) on the cloth. man
in black suit (maroon (red) pocket handkerchief) talking loudly about 'selling short', 'injecting 42 million'.
enter frank zappa telling the truth.

∽

APRIL 15

the lights of trucks at night through the jungle. val on
t.v. (have GUEST STARS in the book). life as dodgems.
no, dr. leary, it's not a film they're making. it's the
struggle between life and mind . . . so why should mind
worry about life? do you see death as the world going
on without you, or you releasing your threads (wires?)
into the world?

∽

APRIL 18

remember getting the white paper on the hola camp
deaths

∽

where is self when I am thinking of it?

∽

APRIL 20

household cavalry doing drill in the sunshine to 'raindrops keep falling on my head'

∽

APRIL 25

For Tom Clark

all my life i've lived before
prose is that
poetry is where at least three times

Well, that takes care of the notebook. It's 11.30. A plane is passing over. I have three cigarettes left and can get no more until 4.30. This morning I woke at six, put on jeans, denim jacket and plimsolls, and began to run. The sun was bright, but it was freezing outside. In places there is still thick snow. I ran down the road, between the pines, to the main gate. On the way back I saw a track beside one of the lakes, and ran along that. Every twenty yards or so I had to stop running and walk carefully across a patch of frozen snow. I pissed into a snowbank and wondered why I couldn't cut a pattern until I realised it was so cold that the piss was almost frozen before it hit the snow. Around the other side of the lake I took a track that led behind a house into a thick grove of pines. The trees had been planted in rows and the path led straight down the middle SHIT I'm going to xerox a copy of this to send to Val so she knows what's happening.

❖

Dear Ed:

Now it's thursday lunchtime. Yesterday I did nothing but

walk around this room, walk around the lakes, lie on my bed. It's the adjustment from things outer to things inner. I read two books: Ed Sanders' '*Shards of God*' and '*Policewoman*' by Dorothy Uhnak.

Well, when I got down to that grove of pines and started to enter the trees a white owl flew straight down the centre of the path and passed directly overhead. At the moment I was looking up, I stepped onto some firm-seeming snow and sank up to my knees. It was the first owl I'd seen, outside of a zoo. In fact I think the only other one I've ever seen was called an Eagle Owl, and is in the zoo at Colchester in a cage whose floor is littered with small dead birds. I was sure I was hallucinating, so, still in the snowdrift up to my knees, I kept staring and yes, it had an owl's face. That set me up for breakfast. Something is happening to my eyes. Looking through my glasses through windows in which trees are reflected I see ghosts everywhere. As if all those who have been here have filled the space with trace. I smoked my last joint before breakfast and sat completely paranoid. There's a Korean novelist here named Kim whose eyes are good to look through. He was telling how he'd learned English from old movies. Like Shirley Temple's "You have to ess em eye el ee / to be aitch ay double-pee why". Then the first time he left Korea and landed in America he saw a newspaper with enormous headlines saying SHIRLEY TEMPLE DIVORCED and thought "Ohhhhh ... these people BLIND!" The only problem with the movies was that kissing was never shown, so the plots suddenly jumped. Then someone else

[87]

started to talk about an SDS girl saying "Communism is good / Capitalism is bad" . . . and a novelist from the South said "What *tahm* of *deh* was it? Oh . . . *mah*nin' . . . I thought if it was the ahfter*noon* she maht hev bin *hah* on some o that marijoo*ahna*." So I went to my cabin, lit the stove, and wrote picture postcards of the Saratoga Racetrack to the children. Later I went up to the house and called David and Nicole, whose voices were good to hear. When I got back to the cabin the air inside was burning and there was a sweet smell of woodsmoke in the room.

Yesterday morning I was woken by the sound of running water . . . a leaking gutter above my window. I'd slept through the alarm, so no time for a run. At breakfast there was a letter from my father. Put it in:

Dear Tommy, Wherever you are when you read this, we hope all goes well. We were very pleased to get your letter, and it was kind to send the book so carefully packed (I almost threw away the letter written on the cardboard). We read it with interest (including the laudatory words on the back of the jacket) and hope it will add to your reputation. I shall try to get the Penguin book in May. There seems to have been a poetry explosion, and the resulting poeticised particles are too small for me to handle mentally with any satisfaction. Sometimes I seem to hover on the edge of a meaning to these minutiae of sensibility, but finally it eludes me. Perhaps it is a private world that I am not supposed to enter. A pity, because beauty does not lose by being shared. I hope you will not think of us as James Joyce thought of his aunt. He sent her a copy of *Ulysses*, and waited for her comments. Apparently nothing was forthcoming. So he wrote to her, and I quote: "There is a difference between a present of a pound of chops and a present of a book like *Ulysses*. You can acknowledge receipt of the present of a pound of chops by simply nodding gracefully, supposing, that is, that you have your mouth full of as much of the chops as it will conveniently hold: but you cannot do so with a large book on account of the difficulty of fitting it into the mouth."

We have not heard from Bridie recently, but I telephoned the hospital yesterday evening and they said she was quite comfortable.

We hope Valarie and the children will enjoy the little change at Brighton. Valarie, I expect, will be back in Colchester in time to cope with the census form.

I had a nasty attack of gout last week, my foot felt like a hot sponge filled with needles, but it has eased off now to a lukewarm tingling. Thank the Lord for that. I have a theory that walking is good for it, especially in the sweet spring air with the trees just breaking into leaf. I am in no hurry to exchange my lease of life for a freehold in eternity, There is plenty of Plato to read, and then I would like to have another go at Plotinus (in a marvellous translation by Stephen McKenna, an Irishman). Your mother is at present absorbed in Treasure Island. She is truly omnivorous. I believe if I gave her the London Directory she would read it (and then complain that there wasn't much plot in it).

We had a letter at Easter from Margaret, the Poor Clare. She seems very happy, and was called in from her wood-chopping to take a telephone call from her father and mother in Australia.

There is a nice show of daffodils and hyacinths in the garden, with tulips and bluebells coming on. Your mother loves to look after the flowers, and I begin to think they love to see her.

I shall type the address in caps as I don't know if YADDO is the name of a person or a place or the initials of an organisation.

We do hope you will be able to find time to see us on your return. We scarcely recognised you from the photograph on the back of the book. I must have been thinking about your poems when I went to bed last night, because I dreamed that you had exploded Bridges' "London Snow" and I was trying to reconstruct it from the particles. Not a dream really; only the mind toying with a theme for a moment and then dropping it.

I enclose a bit of Old England — mind it doesn't disinte-grate on exposure to American Air. (Enclosed was a news-paper clipping of a photograph of an old man in a top hat and knitted scarf, leaning on a stick. The caption read: 'Robert Morvinson, carrier and shoemaker of Stallingborough, Lincolnshire, photographed in 1857 aged 82. This is one of 159 photographs in "A Country Camera, 1844–1914" by Gordon Winter (David and Charles £2.25). Morvinson was born in 1775 when Bonnie Prince Charlie was still alive.') Living with such a collection of characters must have been a perpetual feast. Carlyle used to order a box of long clay pipes from Paisley and smoke a new one every day, putting the old one on the doorstep, before he went to bed, to be taken by who would.

May God bless and direct you. With all good wishes.

I've just realised why I added that. About a year ago, when Stuart was asking me what I'd done "about part two of 'A Serial Biography'", I had the idea of typing out every piece of incoming mail for three months and sending it to him. But then for the first week all I got were bills and invitations to subscribe to TIME and LIFE, so I got bored. But the idea's been lying around there ever since. Well, dust it off, turn it around, take a photograph of its reflection, buy it a set of re-treads and off it goes again. Or maybe it was my lunch today: two pieces of fried chicken, some lettuce and slices of carrot, a tub of cottage cheese and some coffee — all packed in a small black tin lunchbox. I feel I'm still waiting for my soul to catch up with me. It certainly wasn't there on the Jumbo watching the movie (Peter Sellers and Goldie Hawn in "A Girl in my Soup"). They should still run the Queen Elizabeth, empty but for souls. And fidgeting around on my desk I find a sheet of paper which proves me wrong about yesterday:—

> beer and mind and soul and thought and transmigration of souls. woken this morning by the sound of water running . . . a leaky gutter . . . didn't hear the alarm clock so no run no nothing all day (in the lunchpail was ham and mayonnaise, peanut butter and jelly a banana cottage cheese and some strips of carrot) i lit the stove . . . read 'policewoman' by dorothy uhnak. letter from my parents. walked around through the woods sinking ankle deep in mud and came out behind my cabin . . . red squirrel going up the tree (as i write 'red squirrel' i look out of the window and a grey squirrel runs up a tree). back in the house i lay on the bed and read shards of god . . . today i feel incredibly depressed goddamn it my watch is rusting there's a green stripe on the back of my wrist. my plim-solls are drying on the stove what the fuck am i going to write about i better straighten my table and get down to some damn work tomorrow i can take people in ones and twos but en masse and at dinner everyone's full of shit. take lunchpail back to house and have a shit myself.

Fighting off 'characters' is taking time. The words form themselves into speeches and project faces to say them. It's like some enormous political convention inside my head. And they never rest. Last night I dreamed a book, black, with a title on its cover and opened it and began to read. Treacherous bastards I'm going to cork you in until you understand you're PLOT not CHARACTER.

I remember the first time I saw Val. It was noon, in the canteen of the Wellcome Foundation building, Euston Road. I was sitting eating lunch with Steve Fletcher and she came through the doorway and stood at the end of the queue with a girl called Pam. She was wearing a blue (light blue) sweater and a pale grey gabardine skirt. Her hair was cut just to the level of her chin. I decided to spend the rest of my life with her. My watch IS rusty. I took it off and looked at the back and right underneath where it says STAINLESS STEEL BACK SWISS MADE 10047 is a thin brown line. Bastards. I bet their clocks only go 'cuck' now. So I'm going to wash my hair and take the car in to Saratoga Springs to the post office.

Dear Ed:

This is a cassette of winter 1947 (visual) with a sound track from 1971. I wake in the morning shivering: the linoleum freezes the soles of my feet. The window is covered in ice. I have to breathe on it several times, each intake of breath chilling the back of my throat. He agrees with the Indian novelist that J.D. Salinger is one of the more interesting American writers. Ice cubes click. A refrigerator door shuts. Water sluices from a tap. He agrees to go and have a beer and pizza. Doors slam and a car starts up. I begin to cough. There is a thick rime of ice on the sleeve of my pajamas. It is still dark outside. The streetlamps went off at midnight. The one lightbulb makes my room an orange cube of ice. My mother comes in and tells me to get back into bed. She has black hair and wears an apron with a pattern of bright flowers. She brings two hot water bottles. I get back into the cold bed, pushing one of the bottles down with my feet. Warming my hands on the other I breathe the comforting smell of warm rubber. My father comes in and bends over to kiss me. He hasn't shaved yet, and smells of tobacco. He goes downstairs and begins to rake out the fire. As they wait for the pizza music blasts from the room next door where there is dancing. Another shift: the records are all from the '50s — At the Hop . . . Handy Man . . . Lightning Striking Again . . . Way Down Yonder in New Orleans. I hear my parents talking quietly downstairs. It grows light outside. My mother comes into my room again with some newspaper and sticks and begins to lay the fire. I realise I am ill. That's the only time a fire is lit in a bedroom. Listening to the roar of flames I drift off to sleep. I dream he is talking about their energy terrifying her. And that the room he is in has a row of wooden tables and is crowded with students drinking beer. I dream he eats half a pizza which is overcooked . . . the bread hard as a biscuit. And that the Korean novelist is telling them of a pilgrimage he made as a child, for many days up into the mountains, with no money, standing in the snow at night at anyone's door until given a place to sleep and a little food. Till late one night he arrived at a temple and was taken in and fed. And realised that the young boy with shaven head who served him was a beautiful girl . . . and understood he was in a

nunnery. The head nun telling him that now he was
rested he really must move on to the monastery. That they
couldn't let a man sleep under their roof. And sending to
guide his way the youngest novice carrying a lantern on
a stick, the orange light swaying and reflecting from her
bald head as they crossed the snow. I dream that as he
listens to the story he thinks of a letter from his son which
arrived that morning: —

Dear Dad,

I am writing this letter because I could not get all the
news on a postcard. I am having a great time and yesterday I paid 3/– for a drive in a real go-kart: at the bend I put
the brake on so hard the back end swung out and hit the
wall.

The weather is lovely and sunny and today we are going
to the waxworks (chamber of horrors) and Lisa might
take a photograph. Aram has got over his 'flu by the way.

I hope it's o.k. in America for you. If you see a Hell's Angel
take a photo for me.

I have been out with Gaynor and the family to a café and
the waitress was hopeless; forgot everything. Saw a super
funny cowboy film, began like this. Out in the west there
are many cowboys. Some are good, some are bad. Some
are bad with a bit of good in them, some are good with a

bit of bad in them. This story is about some pretty good bad cowboys. See postcard.

Which has not arrived. I wake up. There is a roaring in the room. My mother is talking quietly to the plumber who is mending a burst pipe. It is the sound of his blowlamp I hear as he pumps up the pressure. He says something to me but already my attention is slipping. I am thinking of the snow outside and wondering how the red fire alarm (Penalty for False Alarm £5) looks against it. I sleep again. And dream that he sleeps in a wicker chair in a small house near Torremolinos and wakes with 142 mosquito bites on his left arm and the left side of his face. He has dreamed of reading a sheet of typewritten paper that says:—

I dreamed I was in the street (at the end); money was stolen in a tin box. I put it through the window of a house (small hole) at the same time I was the policeman who stole the money (a wad of notes) and re-locked the box. I dropped the key down a drain outside King's Cross Station. Waited outside the newsagents—above which was the police headquarters—with a crowd of people, getting bored. London became France. I had an injection. An old french lady took me in to make me a gentleman. I had to find the lavatory in the building to change my clothes. And I had to ask in french, the doorman didn't speak english. I went out to buy a copy of (   ), but there were none in the shop. I noticed a play by (   ), a black author. Then on the street again it was New York

The South and the whites were trapped in a room from which they were escaping one at a time through a window (they thought secretly); but we blacks outside were just waiting for the Police Chief. Whites came. We ran. I couldn't use my white car, but had to get to my wife in hospital (my small black daughter was with me). I stole a coach (another man was (briefly) with me). I clubbed the driver, the other man held back the passengers. I drove the coach to the outskirts of the city. A red light on the front kept flashing, and by pressing two red buttons I could stop it momentarily. There were only six or seven passengers at the back. I worried that the radio would transmit. Cut. I was walking back to the coach. When I opened the door it was filled with people and I knew the driver had gone for the police. We mingled with the crowd and, while crossing the first street, I saw the police station with, outside, the driver talking to policemen (each wearing a different coloured raincoat). It seemed easy for them to find one black man and a small girl with pigtails. I went into the subway, but there was only one line, along the eastern edge of the city, and no transfers. The chart was a map of the city covered with trees.

I wake again and it is night. My father is home from work and sits on a chair beside my bed. A wooden chair with a curved back and a seat of plywood patterned with small holes. He switches on the light and begins to read to me from "What The Moon Saw".

The dream was over, and although he understood that

with the half of his mind that had paused to wonder why he had begun the sentence, he knew that the letters had to go on and on to the end . . . like the glass circling and circling the ouija board . . . an order of ritual that would cease only when the green gulls, finishing their last flight, circled for the final time and landed, breaking their legs on the sheet of thick plate glass stretched two feet above the ground. Oh, the surprise on their faces when the gas jets lit beneath the glass and they sizzled their way to eternity. That's all it is.

I found a dead mouse in the woodpile today, curled among some leaves. I thought at first it was asleep, or hibernating, but when I lifted it it was still. I've moved it onto the window ledge beside the catch while I think what to do with it. The more formless I try to be, the more objects push themselves into a shape. I went up to the house a few minutes back to make some phonecalls . . . talked to Harvey . . . then no reply from your number, or from Tom Clark's. So I went into the library to check on that "London Snow" poem. I found a collected Bridges on the shelf, and as I was reaching for it something distracted me. When I opened the book I had in my hand I read Chief Joseph:—

> Hear me, my warriors; my heart is sick and sad
> Our chiefs are killed
> The old men are all dead.
> It is cold, and we have no blankets;
> The little children are freezing to death.

Hear me, my warriors; my heart is sick and sad.
From where the sun now stands I will fight no more
                                        forever!

We are exactly on the borderline of the seasons. This
morning there was snow; now the sun is out and warm.
Through the window I see the blue smoke from my chim-
ney blowing down through the trees towards the highway. I can't hit any rhythm yet . . . I feel like an android. Or
a car that's been converted from petrol to natural gas. Last
night I clearly remember dreaming that I found a bag of
cocaine in the hem of my blanket but someone knocked it
from my hand. It fell onto a piece of white carpet, and I
was down on my hands and knees picking all over the
white fluff sniffing at my fingertips.

Every stupid remark I've heard resurfaces and demands
another hearing. The schoolteacher in London who was
having small children write poems (she was 'modern' . . .
that's the only good thing about sociology: it's really given
the enemy a bright red uniform. It may not show their
own blood to them when they're hit, but we're fighting in
the forest now so we can see them coming and there's
time to get away) and told me "You know, some of them
turned in these RHYMING POEMS. I said 'Children . . . you
will write FREE VERSE!'" Or the women's lib girl at the
University telling Val "You CAN'T be happy doing that . . .
you MUST go out and see some FOREIGN FILMS!" Or Dudley
saying he believed the most important things in life were
"manners, decorum, and style" as if he knew what any

one of the three words meant. The room is filled with a golden light. Tall trees clatter their branches in the wind. Beside me the stove crackles and occasionally pops. I think I'll leave it there.

❖

Dear Ed:

Put in the paper and burn off. So after dinner last night the talk got down to Universities and Grades and The Differences between the French, English and American Systems of Marking. That's the formal penance for being inside your head all day. And people were conscientious. Suddenly Korean voice speak out: "American grades I don like. Students come, they say 'Mr. Kim . . . where I stand?' I say 'You standin in my room, man.' I say to students '"A" is used too much . . . we give other letters a chance.' So I put an "F" and student say 'Mr. Kim . . . have to show this to my parent.' I tell him '"F" mean FINE when I put it: and "A" mean Awfully Anaemic.' Girl come to me she say 'I pregnant' I tell her 'Don WORRY . . . I give you all A's.' Boy tell me his father die, I say 'You just bring me one sheet of writing, you have A.' As he turn to go I see hole in his shoe. 'Forget about sheet of writing' I tell him. American teachers come out of room waving hands saying 'Not enough time . . . I need more time to tell them everything.' I go into class: after twenty minutes nothing more to say. They read essays so CAREfully, making little marks and comments. I read through all of it fast and if I don like, I put B.S., bullshit, on the bottom."

Pouring with rain. I have to get some more logs for the
stove (it's called, by the way, VOLCANO 222). No postcard
from Lloyd this morning. "This story is about some good
bad cowboys. See postcard." is almost as irritating as a
telegram saying IGNORE FIRST TELEGRAM. So let's get in
to something else. I walked back from the house looking
down at the pine cones. How ridiculous to see everything
from where your head is. Fibre-optics should make it
possible to have spectacles like antennae . . . now moving
along one inch from the ground, looking right and left at
your own feet . . . now looking ahead with one and behind
with the other . . . now looking down on the top of your
head. Or how about stretching them out in front of you,
then turning the tips and watching yourself walk forward.
That would really make the background move and rinse
out your brain. Form is content stretched to whatever
shape best fits against the backcloth given by time — so
that is the set where the real action is. If time is like a
back-projection of change, then what is the screen on
which it's focus'd? Let's jam the projector and let the
beam burn a bright hole through one still frame of time.
I wonder when the first meeting was arranged. When did
encounters cease to be random? What fool first said "I'll
see you by that rock when the sun next rises"; no, it would
be something like "when you see again after the black-
ness" . . . some shit like that? If I follow this track I'll end
up working out a code of grunts. To use an old form for a
new content is like making the work a mnemonic for children: each small piece of, for instance, the poem, is
fastened down with little boring arrows pointing at it

from all directions. But H-O-M-E-S is not the Great Lakes.
He said boringly. Let's break out of that.

I got up to measure this room, to start describing it. Seven
easy paces from door to stove: eight the other way, from
wall to wall. But then I caught myself whistling the first
few bars of Dizzy Gillespie's "Night in Tunisia" over and
over again. Somewhere that tape had been switched in. I
remember the first time I really heard jazz was around my
second year in grammar school. That would be '51 or '52.
How strange . . . I'm trying to think of the names of the
two boys who had the records. I can see them clearly—
even to the burn on the smaller one's arm where a Verey
Flare he'd found during the war and lit with a match
exploded. But all I can remember is CHUCK and HANK
which they chalked on the upturned peaks of their school
caps. The school had a semi-compulsory Music Society.
Very straight. I can smell the polish and feel myself wrig-
gling in my chair as another chunk of cultural fudge was
pushed my way. Then Chuck came in with a record . . . I
can see the red and white label now . . . and said it was a
new work by a young French composer named Gilles Spie
called "Le Champ". He explained how, if everyone listened
carefully, mice could be heard moving around in sheaves
of corn. Everyone bent dutifully forward and then this
beautiful noise burst out of the speaker. The unexpected
expression of a truth I'd always known. Bullshit! What a
pretentious sentence. Like "The wind of time blows
ripples across her face". I'll have to be more careful.
They're trying sneak attacks today. And of course it was

through going to jazz clubs later that I smoked my first dope. That would be '55 or '56. A ten-shilling packet of grass I got from Dave Robinson who got it from a spade in the Americana Club (underneath the Mapleton Restaurant, Leicester Square) called Shiny, or Snowy ... one of those names. No, not Snowy: I remember he was one of the gang from the Elephant. Once I saw him run a sharpened nail-file down someone's cheek outside the Lyceum. Dave Robinson looked like a cross between Humphrey Lyttleton and Andrzej Pluskowski. He married a girl named Jeannette who'd inherited some thousands of pounds and went into the property business. It was Dave who took me to the Star (known as the Scar) Club, and I was so gauche I ate the curled-up sandwich that was left permanently on the table so they could serve drinks after hours 'with food'. So, by 1957 I was working in London all day, getting the train home, changing my suit, getting the train back to town, spending until 2 a.m. in the clubs, catching the milktrain (that went first to Gravesend, at the mouth of the Thames, and only stopped at my station at 4 a.m. on the way back to London), sleeping until 7: then the whole round again. Eating methedrine tablets by the handful and weighing 120 lbs. I remember giving Vic Schonfield 200 methedrine in a Zube Cough Sweets tin outside Bush House so his friends could compare them with dexedrine. No, John Lennon, you were not alone. That would be about the middle of 1960 ... no, early 1961. I met Vic through Pete Brown, and Pete Brown through Michael Horovitz, and Michael through Anselm Hollo. And I know I met Anselm in January 1961 because Val was in hospital having Lisa. And how all that started was again through jazz. Sometime in 1958 I went into Zwemmers in Charing Cross road and bought a copy of *Evergreen Review* 2 because it had an article on jazz in San Francisco. I walked down Charing Cross Road, crossed Strand, bought a ticket to Welling, walked to the end of Platform 2, out into the sunshine and began to read.

It's the next day. I find this in my typewriter and look up. Outside the window a small bird is walking down a vertical tree trunk. My ignorance worries me. I think I don't know the name of any tree, of any bird. I sit in this room surrounded by things I can name ... thermos, photograph, jacket, pen, stove, lamp, chair ... and through the ten windows as I swivel round I see things I can only group as 'trees' and 'birds'. But the squirrels save me.

The pine needles on the snow have the same pattern as hairs that stick to the bowl after shaving. I walk through the woods with Kim, who's leaving tomorrow. "Everybody want to be last thief" he says. "Take land from Indian, but then hold on tight." A car pulls up with four men in it. "This road go all the way round?" the driver asks. Then "You Japanese? ... oh ... I was in Korea. Where you from?" "D.M.Z." Kim answers. We walk through the rose garden and across the lawn. Where the snow has cleared the grass is pressed flat; it's like walking over slightly damp shredded wheat. He gives me half a jar of Maxwell House coffee and some slices of chicken.

Dear Ed:

Adrift and alone for two days now inside my head with
no shore on which to land. Speed pushes mind around in
time until the scabs break off and the raw meat of thought
flinches. I saw Ralphy in that small hot room on 8th Street
with Roz and Pauline sitting me down on the bed, giving
me a tumblerful of whisky in my right hand, a joint in
my left, rushing over to the stereo and coming back with
headphones, putting them on me, then all of us laughing
for minutes as he realised what he'd done, and I sat there,
hands, mouth, nose and head full. I saw the Pacific again
for the first time as I ran down the beach drunk, at one
in the morning, away from the lights and towards the
sound of the waves. Ran straight into the sea so that for
days I could taste salt and my jeans shrank and stiffened
and had to be thrown away.

as light has speed we are always

visually in the past   as you read

lettuce   this page may be a lettuce

I wandered around the grounds and the buildings, writing
THE END with a stick in snow banks. Then I went into

the house, and in a nest of drawers found a stereoscope and hundreds of pictures. I spent two hours staring into those worlds, picking the sepia pictures at random. Going from "10802—Snow-Crowned Popocatapetl and Ixtaccahuatl Guarding Cathedral, Puebla, Mexico." (Keystone View Company, Manufacturers and Publishers, Medaville, Pa., St. Louis, Mo. Copyright 1900 by B.T. Bingley), through "13319—The Flower of Venezuela's Regular Army" and "11064—Killing The Fatted Calf, Palestine", to "Cuban Lovers—Courting Through The Barred Windows" (Underwood and Underwood, Publishers. New York, London, Toronto-Canada, Ottawa-Kansas. Works and Studios—Arlington, N.J., Littleton, N.H., Washington, D.C. Trade Mark SUNSCULPTURE). Some of the pictures had texts on the back:—

In legendary tales of Puebla's (Poo-a-blah) birth, we read how this delightful spot was first made known to its founder in a wonderful dream which pictured the real, not in fancy, but as God truly made it, a beautiful plain bordered everywhere by the enrapturing splendor of mountain majesty.

With a population of 90,000, Puebla is classed among the principal cities of the republic in thrift and size. So profusely is it studded by beautiful old churches with massive walls and towering domes of various colors, that by many it is well called 'The City of Churches', but it is more commonly known as 'The City of Angels'.

Save the Capital, no other city of the Republic has seen more of the vicissitudes of war, and between 1821–67 it was captured and occupied six different times—by Iturbide in 1821, by Scott in 1847, and was the scene of Zaragoza's victory, May 5, 1862, when with 2,000 men he repulsed 6,000 French soldiers, who re-entered the following year only to be driven out and captured by General Diaz April 2, 1867.

From here can be seen three of the world's greatest extinct volcanoes, Popocatapetl, Ixtaccahuatl and the peak of Orizaba.

or

The father in the story of the Prodigal Son was so glad at the return of his lost boy, that he prepared a feast for him. He ordered him to be clothed in a new garment, to be adorned with a ring on his hand. For the feast he ordered the best which the house could offer, to be prepared, the fatted calf. The parable intends, of course, to show the feelings of the Heavenly Father for the returning sinner. This picture may give us a better understanding as to what the procedure was in slaughtering the animal. The animal is first caught and bound, and then killed.

No. It's still a day for drifting—but in a submarine through the many-coloured swirling oils. If it's done with truth and love and no wish to profit, in any sense, then it will take shape. The final thing I find in any art that moves me is the clear message 'there is no competition because I am myself and through that the whole'.

This morning I come back to the page and that last part is too maudlin. But I feel low, so let's keep on with it. I've just eaten an orange and put the peel to dry on top of the stove so I can smell it. I put Clara Bow in the window; that way I can read both sides. This morning I had a letter from Marco Antonio, part of which says:—

> I've sent you my long book, *Collected Poems*, to the University. Here it has been received with much verbal enthusiasm, but little written criticism. I wonder if it was worth the trouble, and the twenty years I spent writing it.

and he knows as he writes that the whole point is that there are no rewards. The pain, the depression, the loneliness are the flesh of the oyster: that's what poets taste like. And the relief is when a fleck of sand enters and the layers of pearl start building, taking your attention away from your self. There is no feedback from where we are . . . nothing ahead that can throw back an echo. We sit in silence waiting for the faintest sounds, which are the fragments of the name of god. And when they rise, we follow wherever they lead. As last night I followed them into the library, pulled down Maritain's *Creative Intuition in Art and Poetry* (and when else would I even look at a book like that?), opened it at random, and started reading a poem of Hart Crane's: —

> Yes, I being
> the terrible puppet of my dreams, shall
> lavish this on you—

I live in a country whose poets are afraid of the dark and the wind because they carry burning books outside, which are soon blown out. They have forgotten how to carry a coal, which gives more light as the wind blows. Even the best of them withdraw from what they know they should do. The crack is there in front of them, but they're not sure if they could survive on the other side. They wait for a messenger to arrive and face them: to read out a list of houses, flats, bus schedules and the prices of canned foods. Every day the gap widens . . . and there are no poles left with which to vault across, no planks over which to crawl. Because the trees have long ago been cut down and made into paper for the books they thought would light their way.

You see this is not spontaneous . . . it is talking when there is talk there. Kerouac was the last to try to get all the way round before the bell rang for time. I sleep much more heavily here: the characters and words will somehow act their parts.

❖

Dear Ed:

Art is making new games, that's the message for today. Let me tell you about my regular life here. I've trained myself (now that's a ridiculous phrase) during the past week to wake at five to seven. At seven o'clock I start running past the garage, down through the woods and around the lakes. I am back at the house at 7.15. I wash, make my bed, and walk to the garage building for breakfast. Each day I have a glass of orange juice, cornflakes with cold milk, two scrambled eggs and two cups of coffee. Then I leave any letters I've written in the basket by the door and collect any that have arrived. I walk back to the house, read the mail in my bedroom, go down to the kitchen to collect my lunchpail and thermos, then walk to my cabin. There I clean the ashes from the stove, light the fire with the paper bags yesterday's food was wrapped in (plus any scraps from my wastepaper basket) and some kindling from a cardboard carton. I then read my mail again, by which time the kindling has caught and I can put a couple of logs into the stove from the rack in the corner. I usually look out of the window for a while, at the trees and birds and squirrels. I crumple up whatever cake or cookie is in the lunchpail, and throw it out the door. Then I listen to the traffic for a while. I can just see the highway through the trees. After that I sweep the floor and write letters. At four o'clock I take my lunch things back to the kitchen and read in my bedroom until five thirty, when I go down to the kitchen, make a drink, and take it into the library. Dinner is at six thirty. Back to the house at eight. Make some phone calls. Drink some more. Go to bed. At least that's the theory. Well, we're all going to die, that's for sure. Like the mouse that hasn't moved.

Names and shapes are getting used up fast, that's why the gap is growing. And anyone left on the other side will be inside a faulty machine. As the child grows and the parents die, so does the machine we are in produce its successor. It isn't self-repairing. It wants to die, and any attempt at patching it up turns its wrath against the repairers. When, by a series of coincidences, I walk into the lounge at the airport in Toronto and sitting in front of me is Jean Blondel, last seen in Colchester, you can't kid me that the machine hasn't momentarily run out of new shapes and had to flash him in there. Like going in to town yesterday evening to post a letter to you and first passing a truck with DORN in large letters on the side; then turning a corner and parking beside an oil-drum with DIVERSEY stencilled on it. Like Bradley and Barnett being two players in a basketball game I watched on t.v. And Barnet being the place where Peter Bradley (I still owe him £50) lived when we met. And where we lived for three years six years later. And in the same street: Manor Road. He was a bio-chemist, but had a few sidelines like making a liquid methedrine and barbiturate mixture, making his own drink from pure alcohol and orange peel, and growing his own grass. That was the only stuff I've ever hallucinated on. He didn't know how to dry or cure it, so he chopped it into fine pieces (like mint for a sauce) and we smoked it like that. 1959. You had to smoke about

[111]

a pack of twenty, but then it hit you like a train. I liked him. He was quiet, bright, and pleasant. But his parties were boring: candles, Dylan Thomas, traditional jazz and Greek folk music records. It was at one of his parties that I met Jeff Nuttall. (By the way, it has to be nomadic over the gap . . . so the luggage will be much lighter.)

He stops to watch the smoke rise from his cigarette and to scrape back his chair. Looking to his left he reads on a yellow pad with thin blue lines 'Lewis: 2031 B.Oak St. Sa.Fran. 94117.' The fire cracks once. Outside the window to his right leaves blow and four dark birds peck amongst them. As he looks, and thinks of that sentence, a brilliant red bird lands on a pine tree. The first brightly coloured bird he has ever seen free. 'Cardinal' comes into his head, and on the yellow pad he writes 'cardinal?' He taps the tip of his pen on the desk, then begins a little drum solo. Putting his cigarette in the glass ashtray to the right of the typewriter he drinks his coffee.

In 1955 Ray Collingwood and I decided to go to sea. We got on a trolleybus (696) down to Woolwich and went into the docks. For an hour or so we wandered around, looking at the cranes and wondering why there were two men's lavatories, one marked ORIENTALS. We boarded a couple of ships, talked to a few people, but no-one would take us on. There was conscription then, and a lot of boys had gone into the Merchant Navy to avoid the Army. Although you had to stay in until you were, I think 26, to avoid military service completely. So there was now a law that you couldn't join if you were over 17. We ate lunch in the dockers' canteen, talked a bit, then decided that if we had to do our two years in whichever branch of the Army we were pushed into, we might as well volunteer for three years, get more money, and choose what we wanted to do. Outside the docks we caught a bus to Blackheath (can't remember the number) and went to the Recruiting Office. It was around the corner from my old school, next to the shop where two years before Brian Simmonds, Kevin Considine and I used to spend our dinner money on those round chocolate truffle cakes with tiny chocolate needles all over them. I completely forget what happened to Ray, but the Sergeant explained to me all about travel and then asked me what I wanted to join. The Parachute Regiment, I told him. He told me I didn't weigh enough. When I came out of the office I had a medical appointment, and a place reserved in the Rifle Regiment. But I never took it up. At the medical the doctors found I had a hole in my heart and I spent the next few months on the dole waiting to go into hospital.

I was friendly with Brian Simmonds because he liked Science Fiction. We had our trousers (1954) narrowed to 14" bottoms and bought slim-jim ties in Lewisham Market. Black, about an inch and a half wide, with thin diagonal lurid violet stripes. After a week we were called up one morning in Assembly, and our clothes were pointed out as not the way the school uniform should be worn. But we didn't change, and they said no more. There were two boys with red hair in the class: a fat one named

Brendan Murphy who impressed me one day by bringing his father's Beretta automatic pistol to school in a handkerchief and letting me click it a few times. And a boy called Raven who had a seemingly inexhaustible supply of money. His parents must have had a shop, I'm sure, and he must have stolen from the till. Because he wasn't rich ... not with those bright blue double-breasted suits with 24″ trouser bottoms. We would skip school at the eleven o'clock break and take the train from Blackheath to Charing Cross. Then in Lyon's Corner House we'd eat an enormous lunch, surrounded by middle-class middle-aged ladies, while a string quartet played behind some palms. That was when I began to drink. We thought cocktails were sophisticated, so we'd order maybe three different ones through the meal. Manhattans ... Sidecars ... the very names were so sharp. Later we'd go to the pictures and catch the train that would get us home at the usual time. I would do anything to avoid school that last year. It drove me mad to sit in the classroom. I was going out with a girl named Pat who lived in the next street and whom I'd first kissed during a game of Postman's Knock at a party in the house next door when I was twelve. At eight o'clock I had to leave my house to catch the bus (89) to Blackheath. She went to school at Bexleyheath, about ten minutes away by trolleybus (696 again). So I'd hang around until eight thirty, walk her to the bus-stop, ride in to Bexleyheath and walk her to school. Then I'd go over to the golfcourse and sit for a while ... or walk along the Broadway looking at the shops. At noon I'd go back down to school to meet her, and we'd go to the golfcourse and neck. In the afternoon I'd take the bus back to Welling to read in the Reference Library until four thirty, when we'd meet at the bus-stop and walk home.

The point must lie where 'like' slides into 'is'. I found the epigraph for this book late last night in Trelawny's *Recollections of the Last Days of Shelley and Byron*: —

> Infidel, jacobin, leveller: nothing can stop this spread of blasphemy but the stake and the faggot; the world is retrograding into accursed heathenism and universal anarchy!

Yes, the wheel turns full circle: but the flaw in the rim touches the ground each time in a different place. And for ten years all I have done has been an adolescent's game, like the bright feathers some male birds grow during the mating season. I look at the poems and they make a museum of fragments of truth. And they smell of vanity, like the hunter's trophies on the wall ('I shot that poem in '64, in Paris'). I have never reached the true centre, where art is pure politics.

It is two in the morning, one day in 1964. I am sitting in the fluorescent glare of the canteen at the top of the Faraday Building, near St. Paul's Cathedral, where the Continental and International Telephone exchanges are. I'm talking to Viv Nixson, who went through the Continental training for 13 weeks with me, and to Gene

Mahon who works in International and whom I met once, years before, when he went out with a girl called Joan Finch who sat opposite me in an office in Euston Road. Years later Viv will be the manager of the Victoria Theatre, Stoke on Trent, and Gene will design the label for the centre of Apple Records: but now we are exhausted. We've been working since 5.30 the previous evening: a duty which should have finished at 11, but we extended it (for the overtime) into an all-night . . . which means until 8 a.m. During the night we have a break of two hours, from midnight until two, or from two until four. At the corner tables groups of Mauritians are playing cards. To work in Continental you must speak reasonable French; as the Mauritians do, and have dual nationality, many are here. At 2.30 we go down to the basement and play snooker. The light over the green table, the click of the balls, are relaxing after the flashing red, green, white and orange lights of the exchange and the glare of the canteen. At four I go back upstairs. Several operators are sitting at their positions around the multiple. A couple of supervisors are talking softly at their table in the centre of the room. I am working Ship to Shore, in the corner. Plugging in my headset I lean on my left elbow, hold an answering cord ready in my right hand, and try to doze. A supervisor shouts "One up!". I look at the multiple and a white light glows for a second or two, then vanishes. I hear an operator down the room say sleepily "Continentalservicenumberplease." At eight the previous night, when the exchange was ablaze with lights from incoming calls, a subscriber would have had to wait perhaps ten minutes

for an answer. Now, early in the morning, when everyone should be asleep, there's no delay. The supervisor's
keenness reminds me of the union official who said to
me when the postmen were working to rule and conse-
quently the telephone system was flooded with calls,
"What . . . and lose all this overtime!" when I mentioned
some vague idea of solidarity. But I liked the job. Apart
from the usual Civil Service shit, and the 200 different
varieties of ticket to fill out for calls, you were left pretty
much to yourself. I would 'accidentally' disconnect people
whose tone I didn't like or who were rude to me. I'd let
girls phoning their soldier boyfriends in Germany for
three minutes from a call box (over 10/–) talk for perhaps
ten, instead of cutting them off. One Christmas I linked
the East Berlin operator to the West Berlin operator (there
was no direct link then) and left them connected all
evening. And there were always interesting calls to over-
hear. If you ever call abroad through the operator at three
in the morning and the volume gradually drops, picture
ten bored operators with nothing to do but overplug your
circuit, sit back, and listen. We invented games to pass the
time. A telephone number picked at random would be
handed round, and in turn, at one hour intervals, we'd call
the number and ask for Joe. At eight in the morning,
whoever made the last call would say "This is Joe . . . any
messages?" For a month, every time I worked all night I'd
ring the British Embassy in Paris on one line, Orly airport
on the other, then pull back the monitor key and listen
to them argue about who'd called whom. At four in the
morning. Or we'd find a number with a tape-recorder

connected (like Westminster Abbey at night) and fill the tape with scraps of conversation, the weather forecast in French, the time signal from Norway, and pop records you could dial on certain German numbers. Back in 1964 the phone rings on the supervisor's desk. It is 7.30 in the morning. I'm called over, pick up the receiver, and hear Val. She tells me a letter has just come from the landlords and we're to be evicted that morning.

Sunday is Sunday everywhere. Even here, isolated, the difference must be made: breakfast is at 8.30 instead of 8. In the New York Times Magazine there's a piece about the 'new relevance' of comic-books which, to illustrate its point, says something like 'Students at Yale read extracts over their radio station' . . . which seems to be the opposite of what the man thinks he means. I pin up a few things on my wall: a poster for a reading by Tom Veitch and Clark Coolidge . . . your drawing of the S.S. Panama. The day after tomorrow David is driving over from Northampton to take me back there for a couple of days. I remember when we met, in Anselm's flat in the summer of 1961, he was just beginning his doctorate at the Sorbonne. Now, on the phone, he tells me it's finished; he's just completed the bibliography. So the sixties are over at last. I am back in the exchange. Our evening shift ends at ten, ten thirty, or eleven. If we're not busy, we're released ten minutes earlier. I discover that if I touch the tip of my answering cord to the edge of a socket, the light above goes out, although the caller still hears a ringing tone. At ten forty five the multiple is a blaze of lights. I run the tip along three rows of answering sockets. Every light goes out. We are released. Across the country people listen to the ringing tone, cursing.

❖

Dear Ed:

It's so grey here. Five days of rain, mist in the mornings. The air in the cabin is green, with small flecks of gold wherever the light from my lamp hits a metal window catch or some other reflecting surface. Through a thin crack in the top of the stove I see the bright flames dancing inside. Trucks pass on the highway I can barely make out through the trees, but my chair vibrates. It feels like Christmas when I was five. I shut myself inside the circle of light and go back to 1943. Dates blow off a calendar . . . a few clouds scud by. I am running up the stairs. The carpet is worn through and the stair-rods chatter in their sockets. On the landing at the top is my uncle Arthur. I have a piece of paper in my hand, my head is burning. "Look!" I say to him, "look what I've written!" He takes the paper, and I remember the poem still:—

> o what fun
> to be a boy
> and have a toy
> i teach my soldiers to fight
> and my lions to bite
> o what fun
> to be a boy

and have a toy

                               the first thing I ever wrote. "Copied" he says, continuing downstairs, "you must have copied it from somewhere—you couldn't have written it." The valves that blew out in my head then are still dead. I shine the torch around over them but they can't be repaired. I feel the wall under my hands, the roughness of the stippled distemper. I taste the powder in my mouth as I bite my nails and try to tell him "I DID write it!" And so I lose my faith in truth. Well, everyone you punch at is the same shape. Maybe that, in some perverted way, is why I keep the dead mouse on my windowsill.

timber   truck   vibrates

             my   s   pine

                                 is how I'd write it now, I suppose.

One year later, 1944, at school. I go into the lavatory from the playground to piss. Three boys I've not seen before are standing just inside the door. "Here" one of them calls to me "have you ever seen a match burn twice?" Interested, I go over. He strikes a match, blows out the flame, and presses the hot tip to the back of my hand. I scream. They run off laughing. I lose my trust in people. Well, from the point of view of shadows, there is no light.

i lose
my faith
in truth
i lose
my trust
in people

I suppose it would be now.

Let me send you a copy of a novel I wrote last year (if I sent
it before, this is where it belongs). It's called: —

PLASTIC SPOON   a novel

t.v. is out of focus, or so the watch swings
i mean he is examining it, taking a cigarette, looking
voice says "the picture of indian face" wind, wind
he hears it behind, swinging bleached out in the window
peddler sings "nothin' . . . i just wanna talk t'yuh"
"come up'n sit'n the (now let i deviate

holding three kings : this is now, seven p.m.
the poem the variations the will the spring the from

∾

blur   blur
what's that?   oh
        sepia screw
take a spin in the focal length

[121]

bicycle days (or: a telegram)
la la la LA la la la la

∼

with a flurry of spoke he whirled on his
machine   gravel spurt
                    we are at large
in the machine, and the colours today
are green (with a dash of yellow at the
centre) rose (with a dash of blue
at the edge) and the colour exactly
between green and blue

∼

dank day   a good day   for english poetray

∼

as light has speed we are always
visually in the past   as you read
lettuce this page may be a lettuce

∼

attaching my klein bottle to my möbius belt i
entered königsberg (later kaliningrad) . . . soon i
would be helping count buffon with his 'needle
problem'

⁓

some of you older children may see
the floors in my argument.   mind the edge

⁓

if this text is a half-tone, imagine it as a line-block:
enter through the 'o' in 'tone' or 'block'. now you
are beneath the page—meet me by the coca-cola
sign, or 'egress'.

⁓

out of step (laughter) normal
for most people (titters) now, in
a crash helmet and boiler suit
(doo doo doo in tuba tones) she
applies a false moustache (apple pie lies)

⁓

what goes on in the real world

⁓

JOIN THE DOTS

∿

he's gone into his self! trails of ash
fragments of paper, stop at the edge
of his sucked outline in air. he
detaches his retina: the guide-dogs
run wild. in his ear he beats out in morse
with hammer on anvil "a roomful
of lettuce rendered into one syringe: the
man who turned yellow drinking carrot juice"

∿

fool who invented the wheel because
he couldn't wait to get there quicker

∿

blur blur   blur blur
what's what's that that!!   oh oh
        crew crew

∿

eight bells   each day polish my bicycle
radio waves pass through bodies
causing cancer   waves of colour t.v.
cause bloodclots   medicine leaves nature
no choice but new diseases
seven bells   one bell   silent typing

[124]

～

my bicycle's shape's $^c_o{}^l a$ i bought it
from a stylite   the shape
of its back wheel makes it uncomfortable to ride

～

blur   blur   coming up fast
it overtakes him as they blend into the window
play with marked watches the set
is switched off the images deviate   life
goes on in the album   for the record
our noises are off

❖

Dear Ed:

It was good to hear you. I'm sorry if I sounded chilly on the phone. Being alone all this time, and fragmenting myself back into the past, I've grown paranoid about the Outside Present. I can cope with letters (in fact I need them very much) and the phone calls I make — but the immediacy of calls coming from outside makes me defensive. And I'm wary about taking anything except the work itself when I'm writing. That's the dope I'm using now. I'm going on the vague assumption that if I can completely and correctly describe my self, then that self will wither and blow away. Unless when you have created your self you die. Or unless we really are the hosts for some other force that sits inside us like the trainee pilot in a simulator — and similarly walks back into the world after the so-real crash.

He remembers the banana in his hand as his palm grows cold.

In February 1971 I get off the train from Colchester at Liverpool Street and walk towards the taxi rank. As I pass the news kiosk a small old man wearing a dirty fawn overcoat and carrying a brown paper bag stops me. "You Jewish?" he asks. I tell him no. "Speak German?" "A little." He gives me a sheet of lined paper, torn from a notebook. On it is written an address in Cazenove Road, Stoke Newington. I walk back with him to the ticket office. In a mixture of German and Yiddish he tells me he has come from Paris, where he stayed two days, and before that from Russia. At the ticket window he takes an old purse from his pocket. There are a few coins in it — perhaps eight or nine shillings. I buy him a ticket to Stoke Newington. Then I realize what he's saying. "Ainun-TswansikYahra." Twenty-one years in a labour camp. I go with him to the barrier, point out the train and tell him it will leave in ten minutes. We shake hands and I walk away. I'm going to the Press to see Barry and sign some books. We meet and go for a drink. He tells me about the old Elvis Presley English Concert rip-off. How a hall was booked, tickets printed, advertisements and posters sent out — all without Presley ever having been approached. Half the tickets were sold straight, and half at inflated prices on the black market. Then it was announced that, unfortunately, the concert had had to be cancelled. The straight money was refunded through the ticket agencies . . . and the money from the black-marketed tickets was pure profit. We go to the Press, smoke a joint, and I look at the stack of fifty books. I tell him I can't sign them and go home.

I remember the pains in the back of my neck and my spine after sitting on the floor for six hours setting type. I remember setting a complete page of a story by Fielding Dawson, getting up, stumbling, and kicking the whole thing over. I remember Val taking copies of the magazine and the books around the stores in a paper carrier bag and being told "Oh . . . we don't take things like THAT . . . we only stock REAL poetry." 1963.

After writing that I went for a walk up to the house to see if the sunlight would do anything. After this week of rain the light this morning hurts my eyes. Up in my room I began to look through a book called *Dancers, Buildings, and People in the Streets* by Edwin Denby, and came across three paragraphs about de Kooning that seem to accurately reflect my feelings today: —

> In the presence of New York at the end of the thirties, the paranoia of surrealism looked parlour-sized or arch. But during the war Bill told me he had been walking uptown one afternoon and at the corner of 53rd and 7th he had noticed a man across the street who was making peculiar

gestures in front of his face. It was Breton and he was fighting off a butterfly. A butterfly had attacked the Parisian poet in the middle of New York. So hospitable nature is to a man of genius.

Recently a young painter walking at night down Third Avenue near 10th Street saw him running fast. The young man wondered why de Kooning was running so fast at night. Then he saw Lisbeth, de Kooning's little daughter. They were playing hide-and-seek.

"I'm not so crazy about my style," he said to me recently, "I'd just as soon paint some other way." When he was in Rome last autumn, he told me, he met at a party an American painter of his age, dignified and well-dressed, with a nice wife and college son. They were making the rounds of museums and the ruins, they knew all there was to see, and enjoyed looking at it intelligently. Bill said that when he was young he expected he would later turn into a man such as that, but somehow it hadn't happened.

I never did describe this room, though I gave you the measurements. The floor is wooden, painted grey, as is the skirting board. The walls and ceilings (high, pointed) are white. The door is in the centre of the wall to my right. It is wooden, stained, as are all the window frames. There is a window either side of the door, two windows in the wall opposite me, two in the wall to my left (between which is the stove), and four behind me. I sit at my desk, facing the centre of the room, on a wooden chair. Slightly behind me, to my left, is a tall metal lamp. Beside it are the log-rack and cardboard boxes of kindling. Between the kindling and the stove are a white metal and plastic chair and a bucket filled with ashes. The stove stands in a wooden tray full of sand, and there is a bent brown metal reflecting screen behind it. To the right of the stove is a bookcase, empty but for an aerosol fire-extinguisher. A brown rocking chair (wood) with a cane bottom stands in front of the shelves. In the left-hand corner of the room, facing me, is a cane armchair, next to a low wooden table with curved legs on which stand a small lamp, my lunch-pail, and a thermos flask (red). Against the wall, between the two windows opposite me, is another bookcase, with a few books on the top shelf and some photographs of Val and the children. A square wooden armchair with an adjustable back and two white cushions is at the centre of the room. In the right-hand corner is a metal day bed with a light green and white paisley patterned cover and a white rough linen pillow. To the right of my desk is a small table with a glass ashtray on it: and, underneath, my waste-paper basket. In the corner behind me, to my right, a small white cupboard with no door holds a broom and dustpan. Beams of sunlight fall across bed and cane armchair.

He is lying on a hospital bed. A nurse has given him an injection in his left arm, and a catheter tube is being inserted into the vein inside the bend of his elbow. He is conscious, but feels nothing. The nurse wipes his fore-head. In the background machines click and whir. He cannot see what is happening: in the silver shades of the overhead lamps he sees only a distorted picture. The tube penetrates further. He feels a tickling inside his left shoulder. Then nothing more. Suddenly his heart kicks. The tube has reached it and is probing inside.

It is a Saturday morning in the spring of 1958. Colin Medhurst, Bob Hawkins, Micky Annett and I walk through Leicester Square. We cross New Coventry Street and go up Wardour Street. Opposite the *Flamingo Club* is an expensive shoe-store. We go in, and Colin buys a pair of dark brown Italian shoes with short pointed toe-caps. Crossing to the doorway of the Flamingo we check who's playing that evening, then walk through Berwick Street market. At the end of Berwick Street, just before it meets Oxford Street, is Sam Arkus, the tailor. Bob is going to pick up a new suit. We go downstairs and he tries it on. It's a dark blue wool/worsted three-button narrow-lapel Italian-style (no seam up the back) jacket: the trousers are cut to 18″ knee, 18″ bottoms, no turn-ups. He looks at himself in the mirror while Toby, the cutter, hovers behind. He turns left side, then right side, then goes closer to the mirror and runs his finger along the left shoulder of the jacket. "Look at this" he says, "a WRINKLE!" Toby murmurs something about it smoothing out with wear. Bob loses his temper. "With WEAR" he shouts. "Three fucking fittings and thirty-five fucking guineas and you tell me it'll smooth out with WEAR! Take the fucking thing apart and do it again by next Saturday." We have a coffee in the Wimpy Bar. Bob is still fuming. "*Cunt*" he says . . ." what does he take me

for? Some fucking SCRUFF?" We go down Charing Cross
Road to Dobells and buy some records. Micky goes to his
alto-sax lesson. Bob goes to see his girl. Colin and I take
the train back to Welling. I arrange to call for him at eight
—we've decided to go to the local dance-hall, The
Embassy, rather than back up to town. When I call round
he's still getting ready: ironing and starching two small
white handkerchiefs into eight regular points for his top
pocket (we scorn the squares of stiff cardboard with neatly
stitched triangles of cotton at the top that are becoming
popular), and re-polishing his new shoes. In the bar of the
Rose and Crown we meet Brian, Micky, and Micky's
brother Colin. He's about 5′4″, thirty years old, with a
brown, almost bald, head.

This book is a book of distractions. I go to get a pack of
cigarettes and my dark glasses. On the way out, I stop to
read, for the first time, a notice on the wall: —

WARNING

DO NOT TOUCH THE EXTINGUISHER

Except When There Is A Fire

. . . .

TO OPERATE

1. Pull out pin on left side.
2. Point rubber at fire.
3. Squeeze handles together.

Through the kitchen window I see Raja, who's been very sick for some days with asthma (it was he who answered the phone to you the other night), and a shape I realise must be his wife (there's a strange blue car with New York plates outside the door). I look across the grass to Curt's house and a short tape flickers through, as it has been doing occasionally since Sunday. The tape starts with a feeling of irritation at my ungraciousness in not taking a slice of Hortense's coffee cake at their house-warming on Sunday afternoon. Then there's a counterpoint of a feeling of how ridiculous it is even to remember that, as I'm sure she didn't notice, or care. A low bass enters, composed of 'she made it herself' and 'they both seem pleasant without being forced'. It ends with a chord combining all these things and saying 'you made a false move'. O.K. Hortense, I'll have a slice of cake. Magnet runs over the tape. At night I can hear the loudspeakers from the Harness Races.

Yesterday I sent Val a copy of Aram's book *Words and Photographs* for her birthday next Tuesday, and I'll try to phone her. There's no tape I can play about her: she just changed the whole machine from mono to stereo.

I was talking about Micky's brother Colin. It was through him, in the middle 50s, that I was cured of my middle-class view of the police. One Saturday night, after a minor fight after a dance at the Drill Hall, Bexleyheath, I saw him arrested and put, unmarked, into a Black Maria. Next morning he appeared minus a tooth and with stitches across his head. 'Fell down the stairs to the cells.' And that trips a key to Dudley standing outside his house in camouflage jacket and combat boots and calling for the police. And thinking the world would be straight if he called them and shut his front door. Hasn't he heard of milk bottles and windows? Doesn't he know the revolution's not coming by mail? Enough. The University Album's not being played today.

He is dressed in a white gown and lies on a trolley being wheeled along a corridor. He is drowsy. Outside the operating theatre the trolley stops, and a doctor in green overalls with a green face-mask leans over and looks at him. He feels hands on his right arm, the chill of alcohol, the prick of a needle. A voice tells him to count backwards from 10. At once he feels wide awake, though his eyes are shut, and thinks 'this is taking a long time to work'. As he thinks 'work' he opens his eyes. There is an enormous weight on his chest; he is inside an oxygen tent. Eight hours have passed and the operation is over. He runs the thought through again: 'this is taking a long time to work'. He can see no break in it. He screams for them to take him out of the oxygen tent—the clear plastic only a few inches from his face seems to be suffocating him. Two days later, when the nurse is out of the room, he forces himself out of bed and over to the table where, in a drawer, is his file. He reads how his heart was stopped, his blood pumped through a machine: how his breastbone was sawn in half, his heart stitched, his chest sewn up. He reads of the pints of blood poured into him, and how, at the end of the operation, after his heart had been restarted, it had stopped again, and how he'd been given massive shots of adrenalin to bring him back to life. Nowhere can he find the key.

I still run that thought through sometimes. Somewhere there must be a flaw in it. Somehow I must find the weak point and snap it. It's too perfect to be human. It tastes of technology. When I wrote 'I feel like an android' I knew what I was writing.

(APRIL–MAY 1971)

THE VEIN

Sitting at a light wooden desk, facing a pale cream plaster wall. To my left, one of the two long windows of the room. Old uneven glass. Dark green outside shutters closed. A small black lamp jutting out of the wall to the side of the desk shines down onto a radio (France Marseille playing something Brazilian) and reflects onto this paper from the two grey steel sheets that cover the bottom halves of the shutters. Beyond the lamp is my bed, double, with a striped red and green cover. Along the wall beside the bed runs a slatted wooden shelf with on it a glass vase next to a painted wooden tomato. The room is L-shaped. Vinyl floor-covering in herringbone light oak. Behind me in the corner (I'm sitting on a straight wooden reed-seated chair) is an armchair covered in mostly grey. In the narrow part of the L, away from the windows are two chairs similar to mine and a wooden table with a white tiled top. Past them is a small bathroom, and a kitchen with sink and refrigerator—no stove yet.

When the shutters are open I look across the street to a patchy yellow wall with two windows edged in white, very small and not level. Leaning out of one usually covered by a small bamboo screen is a young Arab girl, smooth olive face, gold earrings, neck chain caught between her teeth, staring down at a yapping poodle. A pair of bright red shoes lies on the sill. The other window is never open, but frames a cactus in an earthenware bowl.

Sunlight flashed across the seats as the plane banked. Snow-covered mountains to the left. Bus into the city (36f). Early autumn temperature. Down the wide stone steps of the station, right turn into La Canabière, sea in the distance. Reflections from a gilded statue high to my left. Water choppy. Heavy traffic. Cross to the edge of the dock then walk around the port. Back across the road by the Mairie. Right into Rue du Refuge. Up the narrow flight of brown hexagonal-tiled stairs.

> what happens in any
>
> sovereign body is created
>
> on the evidence of the last
>
> head on its last lap
>
> those of us watching
>
> then, during the programme

see the die seem to be cast

to draw the teeth

of our first question

affecting essential interests

they and only they had

she was dealing with

an unworthy family

gathered for death

inconvenient location

gruesome tired mannerisms

a bit thick coming from her

losing the thread of argument

in a sinuous cartwheel

drained of what life

hurried out with a pushchair

unsparing he takes us

to the cabaret

into patterns and groups

contrived for distraction

more likely

to deepen withdrawal

such a decrease

in which women

had views diametrically opposed

soon changes his tune

howling

face to face

cruel for people

recoiling in horror

plastered indeed

by any form of social

charges and interest

it may be healthy

to change the tone

Later, on the phone at the Centre, Franco invites me to
Viozene for the New Year. Out again and back to the
station, this time by a different route. Dark Tunisian cafés,
shops with rolls of bright cloth. By now I'm exhausted.
Not much sleep; the journey; having to adjust quickly to
speaking French. I find the Information Desk and the
woman there (young, pretty, dark hair, very thin, black
dress with silver and gold ornaments, bright red lipstick

and nose almost the same colour from the cold she's sneezing through) looks as irritated as I feel. I explain what is needed and suddenly she asks me if I'm not French. I tell her no, she cheers up, works out the tickets and times for me, smiles and congratulates me on my accent. Walk back feeling happier, last red of sunset fading as I head down to the port, turn left for a stroll. Three whores lean against the wall opposite the Opera House, hands in the pockets of short fur jackets, laughing and talking with a man holding a large german shepherd on a chain.

of administration

in growth dynamics

use of perspective

attachment to things

entail perpetual disruption

of what space is for

built up

in absence

transactions typically occur

under conditions of heightened

variations in taste

spaces, isolated thoughts

which his concept of beauty

distorts to represent

thinking and feeling life

he considers in particular

superimposed spatial images

accelerating production

of different times

to control the future

Dark wet street, mist. No-one about except a white car turning by the Hotel Dieu (lights on) flashing a jolly bass radio voice. The splotches of blood that yesterday led from the kerb up the steps washed away. A cardboard carton that once contained an electric radiator is now in the fountain of two bronze fishes. Steep to the station. Four policemen leave their car parked obliquely across the corner by the steps and go into the Grand Escalier for coffee. Walk through Metro entrance and up the elevator. Coffee (5f) at the station buffet, a drunk next to me dropping his change over the counter into the soapy water. Furthest carriage forward, Quai F. Dark, curtains drawn, man and woman sleeping. She moves, I sit down, doze until Cannes. There an elderly Frenchwoman, fur coat, breezes into the compartment, says firmly "C'est grand jour", throws up the blind and begins to read a newspaper. Grey sky. Sea near the beach the colour of faint green tinted glass. Graffiti ANTIBES in red paint on side of the station wall. Think of Graham Greene. Long pebble beach, a group of cyclists, one runner. A fisherman with four rods out. One small patch of beach covered with seagulls. Sea dark grey at the horizon just before Nice. The sleepy couple leave, a Japanese girl sits in the corner, a couple come in from the next compartment, nervous about reserved seats. He has brown hair, a red moustache, wears a bright green sweater. She has an almost matching green suit. Flash of black lace slip, patterned black stockings, shiny shoes. They share a sandwich wrapped in silver foil out of a battered brown plastic case. "T'es paysanng" he smiles at her as I show how the curtain clips back. Japanese girl ill eight weeks with 'flu in Marseille is going to Vienna. Can't comprehend how I'm here for two months: "such long holiday. . . ?" Tunnels. Only small dim orange lights in the ceiling. The green couple find everything either interesting or funny: "Un suedois", he shrugs as a tall robed black man walks past. At Ventimiglia almost an hour's wait. In the train next to us attendants throw used pillows in an arc down the corridor. Look out of the window after a lot of banging and see a wooden float loaded with batteries being pulled away. The lights come on. We all stare into the first class compartment of a train heading for Marseille: ARIA CONDITIONATA. Two fat Canadian women are complaining about people smoking in the corridor. We move off, past broken greenhouses. "Pas cultivé" sniffs the paysanng. Bordighera. Walkers with black umbrellas on the sea-front.

this book has been edited

to detect the note

of such preoccupations

blue evening light

desire out of stasis

for jobs

investment itself

ruthless traders

organising forces

unable to stop the drift

of imagination over materiality

form an autobiography

in fires of competition

only to emerge stronger

within this system of production

brought into our homes

which in turn form the basis

of generating and acquiring

aesthetic pleasure

conventional these days

An hour by car with Luca and Franco into the mountains, through the cloud and out into sunlight on clean snow. Blue light at the bottom of deep footprints. Drive to Cosio. Narrow steep stone streets. Abandoned terraces. A crib on an outside window ledge almost level with our feet. A white enamel urinal cemented to a wall. Two old women in the snow washing clothes at a communal concrete laundry. Fireworks and champagne at midnight. Further up the mountain, Upega. Posters in Provencal. Tiny shop with thick chenille ropes forming a curtain at the door. Stacks of cardboard boxes marked with their contents: 'Lacci de Scarpi!' An old man scatters grey gravel on the icy path. In the church mandarins hang on the tree instead of lights, the three kings are hidden behind a curtain, sun yellows the top windows. We drink a port standing around the stove with the owner of the only hotel, an old lady with lively eyes constantly rubbing together hands bent with arthritis. She sees the future black. Only 13 year-round inhabitants. Her son, 32, doesn't want to leave, but has no work. He went for a job as a forester but there were over sixty applicants: ". . . people with degrees, doctors, lawyers from Turin. . . ."

       cluttered with illusion

       based on writing

       remixed

       to demolish any narrative

of the world within

no image concealed

from the realm of material

accumulation and circulation

in part as would be true

enduring time

by herself he touches her

surrounded by models

able to pass unrecognised

in the stream of money

implied by a photograph

where the sun never seen

can be constructed

crashing through layer after layer

on a depthless screen

with the requisite speed

Early morning walk with Franco and the dogs. Two kilometers in the silence, the animals afraid of the echoes of their barks. The valley below filled with mist traced with the shadows of the mountains. Yellow markers every hundred metres, violet shadows of trees, water dripping from eaves, running down pipes made of hollowed logs. A lone snow-woman with dry-grass hair on her head, under her arms, at her crotch. Lunch of gnocchi al pesto on the road with Franco, Daniela and Anastasia. The portici of Pieve del Teco. A wooden rocking horse being carried down the hill as we left Viozene. Antonello riding past on a fluorescent bright NEPAL bicycle (Made in Germany). Flickering grey of olive trees. Geese in the bushes as the train pulls out of Albenga. Change at Ventimiglia. Slow Blue Train along the coast to Nice. Empty Lyon Express already in the station. Turn off the heat and light, open the window. Strange feeling of pleasure, of going home, as the train makes the long curve to Aubagne. Vietnamese rolls with lettuce and mint on the walk uphill. In the mountains aspirins take longer to dissolve.

somewhere behind us

thrown into the street

patiently to see

rotting pieces of car

buttons working backwards

against nerve junctions

tilt her head

towards her ankles

in the underground light

black fur gleamed

off the oil drum

searchers found

a delicate bubble of oil

sweeping through it

pure oxygen

dawn touched

at the corners

rose to flame

lengths of thin steel

drawn across dust

The second of January. Number 60 bus, jammed, up to Notre Dame de la Garde. Model ships suspended from the ceiling inside, paintings on the walls given as offerings. Lit candles in red or clear containers. Almost sunset. Soft light, clear to the mountains, the city breathing below.

Late afternoon my first visitor, Nathalie du Pasquier. I make coffee. Pot au Feu that night with her and Angel Darisio at his house in Rue du Panier almost opposite the end of this street. We stand on the tiny roof terrace, a clear cold night, trying to match up Orion and the direction south with a circular dark-blue revolving guide to the heavens. A walk later by the port. Angel enraged with the guard-dog whose sudden bark coincides with Nathalie slipping and falling backwards, the money from her pockets scattering in silver arcs. Drinks at O'Stop. As we walk back down Rue du Refuge a motorcyclist roars towards us, taking his bands off the handlebars and stretching them sideways shoulder-high as we step aside.

shifting in thick

time on

motions playing out

across from me

not in sequence

cut into the sides

of an extension run

below his eyes

were tombstones

ringed with razor-wire

he threaded

bright slashes of colour

through open

jolts of fear

measuring, calculating

shaking so hard

a lump of shadow

watching

turned from side to side

shielding us from the sun

8.30 a.m. Shutters down at Nathalie and Angel's. Low cloud. Try different croissants. 3f. Rue du Panier; 3.20 Rue du Refuge; 3.40 Place de Lenche. In each bakery circular cakes decorated with cherries, angelica and grapes either being made or laid out. La Couronne des Rois. Along Rue St.Laurent grey shutters rolled up on one shopfront reveal heaps of fishing nets. Dodge across the road and past two schooners(?): *Alliance* and *Le Don de Dieu*. A boy in green jacket and jeans, and a man with long black hair, moustache, blue jacket with lighter stripes along the shoulders and down the arms, his trousers rolled at the bottom, are fishing. Round the tip of Fort St.Jean as the sun clears a hole in the cloud and flashes a beam onto a man in denims reading on the stone bench. MA 480150 (white) and MA 568747 (blue) head out to sea. Oil-green rough water. One small boat coming in, sail furled on the cross-tree, outboard putting, the man at the stern with yellow oilskin flung back like a cloak. Phare Ste.Marie flashing red in groups of two. Water clear over the rocks. Second (white) outboard coming in, car-tyre around bow, mast down horizontal. Man wearing a cap, black jacket with blue shoulders, waves as he twists into another dark coat. As I walk around towards the telescope (2f) a third, larger, boat is accompanied in by a flock of swooping seagulls. Too late to read its number. The telescope clicks off and a frogman, olive-green suit and spear-gun, clambers up over the edge of the dock and walks away. Looking in his direction I notice a smudge of brown smoke beyond the building behind the bright green painted light. A clock strikes nine and the ferry NAPOLEON looms out, a pilot boat dwarfed at her side under the RAN of FERRYTERRANEE. An AGS truck pulls up to the bollards. As the NAPOLEON clears harbour the small boat speeds back into the basin. Incoming and outgoing fishing boats pass exactly level with the VIEUX PORT Vitesse Limité a 4 Noeuds sign. Return past the comer of the fort as a dark plank floats in towards the anglers. A pale green plastic bag undulates just below the surface. Past the Impasse des Belles Marinières. Provencal headline: CORSE — briser Ie mur de silence. At the Bar des 13 Coins three red plastic chairs are spaced neatly on the wet pavement. Coffee at Chez Jean. M. Hugo, brown head, white hair at the sides, light blue windbreaker, sits at the end of the bar. In the street outside six policemen (four with green shoulder flashes and cap-bands, one corporal and one sergeant) are noting the numbers of parked cars. M. Hugo leaves the bar and drives away. Sunlight is a low yellow line below fast-moving clouds.

The museum in the Maison Diamantée empty, small dry

black grapes on the vine that spreads over the side facing
the sea. Images of the plague in 1720. A massive painting
of corpses on Montée des Accoules, a line of hooded
monks climbing the escalier of Rue de Moulins. Enormous
iron pincers used to move the bodies. A device to punc-
ture envelopes and letters so they could be purified in
steam. Prints of doctors' clothing: robes to the ground of
animal skin, head completely covered, a long cone like a
bird's beak stretching out from the face filled with scents
and spices. A room on the history of playing and tarot
cards. Another with an exhibition of photos of the mass
deportation from, and destruction of, the Vieux Port by
the Nazis in 1943. A picture of people being shepherded
down steps by the old Customs Building I passed earlier. I
learn that Père Callol of L'Eglise de St.Laurent "sonna le
glas" throughout the event and that the Gestapo headquarters were at 425 Rue du Paradis. Additions to vocabu-
lary so far: *cohue, criblage, pégre, malfrat, truand, loubard.*

        pale green glass

        frames disintegrating tarmac

        down to the tunnel

        of the corner of his eye

        moving on

        to some other

        man for the moment

horizon of empty water

locking him away

inside and he wore

two pictograms

set in strange lines

invisible in air

energetically above them

heels and silk

scatter snow

in the middle of a room

swirling out of the mist

bright with arrangements

tainted too historically

Police cars blocking traffic on Quai du Port. Old woman knocked down almost opposite LE TROU BAR GLACIER sign. I stand looking behind a man in a brown bomber jacket on whose back is the message MANAGER STAFF / UNIQUE BLEND OF RARE QUALITY. There's a trail of blood along the road and onto the white painted turn arrow. A cream Renault 4 (88 24 JH 33) is slanted towards the kerb and two policemen are measuring everything not moving with yellow tape. A man in a dark green sweater, jeans, a leather jacket over his shoulder and carrying LIBÉRATION in his left hand gets out of the back of a parked police car and hovers nervously around the door of the bright red Marin Pompiers truck (3439 MA 13). To my right a woman in gold sunburst earrings is explaining how she was once hit by a bus that mounted the pavement and broke her arm "but the police came and swept the fragments of glass out into the street and swore it happened there." Empty plasma bottles and white-painted toolboxes lie in the road. Another man (red shirt, tweed jacket, brown sweater) gets out of the police car, takes keys from his pocket, goes straight to the Renault and drives it forward to park between a white Fiat Uno (4755 MX 13) and a dark Nissan Bluebird (3908 PA 13). Above the frosted part of the window of the Rescue Truck a white belt jerks up and down as its wearer presses rhythmically on the victim's chest.

Up Rue Breteuil. Sudden flash of mountains looking down Rue Bossuet. Wander around Perier. Black metal wall of Libyan Embassy, green flag above it. At the corner of Boulevard Rivet and Rue du Commandant I notice the ceramic number 15 set into the wall. Along further, number 73's doorway is flanked by two concrete fish and VIVE LE ROI is scribbled in black felt-tip across the EAUX panel. Past the Monastère des Clarisses, the Portugese Consulate, the brass plate for 'Docteur Franck Daniel: Maladies du Systeme Nerveux'. Down into Rue du Paradis. There's a memorial plaque on the side of what must have been 425 but is now a short row of two storied buildings: in order from the corner—a Moulin d'Or bakery, a bank, a florist, a clothes shop, a shoe shop and a tabac. On the windows of the Garage La Mediterranée are sprayed outlines of stars. Stopped at the lights, 6298 MH 13 contains two young men with matching violet shirts with green collars. The earth has turned sufficiently for the head of my shadow to brush the buildings as I walk back towards the centre of town. Soft green patches of pine-needles everywhere this week from Christmas trees put out alongside the plastic bags of rubbish, handles tied into rabbit-ears.

he had forgotten

quite violent fights

listening

to the continuous pounding

of some other thought

looking at the surface

far away down

in a cloud of dust

tattered lace about her

she watched him calmly

bits of it he tore off

at the end of each meeting

seemed colour-coded

sparkling violently

tingling on his skin

holes turned round slowly

in brown earth

lined with age

he smelled burning

trees in darkness

In the Botanical Gardens a tree (*phytolacca dioica* "Belombra") is wrapped in grey felt and tied with string. The slid-back side door of a van parked by the Mairie changes its name to PLICE. A crowd shouts abuse at the driver of a car reversing onto a pedestrian crossing. She gets out, ignores them, pushes her bottom lip forward and enters a Patisserie, leaving a trembling grey-haired old lady in the back seat.

a voice came

from an imaginary telephone

on the dashboard

shrink-wrapped packages

soft underfoot

glowed in the dark

blinds slanted to make

the match flame

blast across his face

snap shut

in the jungle

after the ones still alive

start confessing

flashbulbs go off

her hand flicked back and forth

over a section of floor

he had heard more

than every single word

from the once proud

ruins of arches

Morning. Low winter sunlight slanting through the mists of shoppers' breath in Rue de la République throwing tiny shadows across the goose-flesh of the plucked chickens in the tray outside Boucherie Moustapha. The horrors of FNAC.

Grey morning. Work. In the afternoon to the port: ferry

(*César*) across the harbour. Past the theatre that once was
the auction-house for fish (at least I assume that's what
CRIEE LIBRE DE POISSON in stone letters high across the
facade means). Explore around Bas Fort St.Nicolas. In a car
parked facing the sea at the end of the quai a man's head
(striped shirt) turns towards me. A blonde woman's head
continues to move in his lap. At the dead-end around the
Fort, behind the wire fence, a tiny white wooden dog-
kennel. Further up the hill, a paved circle on a promon-
tory, ringed with a redwood fence. The *Chateau d'If* passes
below as I read the plaque:

JARDIN MISSAK MANOUCHIAN

Chef d'un groupe de resistants en France
1906 — 1944
fusillé par les nazi

to the side, a larger panel:

Les 22 compagnons de Manouchian

Boksov, Rayman, Bancic, Alfonso, Cloareg, Della Negra,
Elek, Fingerwajo, Fontano, Geduldig, Glatz, Goldberg,
Grizwacz, Kubackim, Luccarini, Rouxel, Salvadori,
Schapiro, Tavitian, Usseglio, Wajsbrod, Witchitx.

In the sea below is a stationary single skiff, blue: green
tips on the skulls. A grey and white cat, ears chewed off,
sits on one yellow ochre bench staring at an abandoned

pair of black trousers on another. A black and white cat scrambles up a tree. Walk on up the hill and into the Jardin du Phare. Old people, most with thick glasses chat on benches. One blonde woman is knitting, a white cloth spread on her knees. A dayglo green tennis ball rolls down the hill and is stopped by an elegant Chinese foot and pressed into the grass. Two black boys on roller-skates hurtle down the PELOUSE DANGEREUSE. A long way below, the Fort St.Nicolas couple have left their car and lean on a railing looking down at the sea. A small girl climbing on the monument Aux Heros de la Mer is pulled off it by her mother who shouts "Y'a du vent ici . . . il faut se BUttoner". On the wall of the chateau is a plaque marking the spot where Victor Alfieri's "soul was awakened". MA 43217 comes into port as the skiff is joined by an identical one and in single file they skull into the basin. Walking back on the lower path I pass an old woman in a white headscarf talking to a standing man as she crouches to feed eight cats—one of them the earless—off small polystyrene plates. I catch only "Monsieur Thomas est venu en juang quatre vang neuf." Past the Foreign Legion recruitment office "open day and night", and crossing the traffic loop from the tunnel under the port, standing by the strange circle paved like a chessboard in the middle of the fast lanes, I notice a bright blue and yellow metal bridge stretching behind the buildings to the right. I find my way to it, cross, and arrive outside the Boutique des Santons.

Dawn. White light on the Chateau d'If. Against a black sky

a seagull underlit by the Bonne Année sign. Half moon.
Red flashes in groups of two from the end of the digue.
Glitter of ferry from Corsica or North Africa coming in. An
expensive red sports car parked facing the harbour
entrance blinks its headlights: three short, one long. The
water turns pale blue. My shoe-prints on the marble slabs
in front of the Marseillaise almost violet in the condensa-
tion. Three men are hauling the *Anna* out of the water in
a cradle operated from a hand-held box. One walks backwards in the boat, holding the beam, to drift it into the
loops. They lift, turn, turn again and lower it onto a flat
four-wheeled trolley, rocking the boat to starboard to hold
it steady with a wooden block.

in one outstretched hand

an odd sensation

included balance

working to repair the damage

of triumph on his face

folded against the edge

of exhaust fumes

closing his lids

properly needed great care

she heard a rustle

little numbers

flew around trees

tumbled across a moonlit field

trying to reassemble

his head again

she blinked

some sort of code

subtle variations

in the colour of her eyes

With Julien to Ventabren. At Rognac the building where he was born is now the Municipal library and we find one of his books on the shelf. A Barrett sign for New Luxury Villas where once were olive groves and vineyards. The old olive mill. Wheels rolled in a circular stone groove for cold pressing, then the resulting cake squeezed under warm carpets, the oil channeled into a cistern of water to be scooped from the surface. High wooden bunks where workers slept away from the rats: in use until the Popular Front. Tired. Rest on bed as the room darkens. White cat miaowing through the window behind a small orange tree. Sounds of paper being crumpled, puffing of breath, Julien saying "Hé voila" to himself, footsteps going upstairs, water running, footsteps faster downstairs, wheezing of bellows, then "Ah ... MERDE!" When I wake and go down the fire is blazing. Pizza with Catherine and Jeanne.

Cemetery at Ventabren. Cold wind in the hills. A bank of concrete slots, two sealed with metal doors. A typewritten note in an empty one:

Commune de Ventabren
la fosse commune contenant les restes mortels de
M. Durand, Paul
inhume(e) depuis 1947
devant etre restituée a la Commme
la Famille est priée de se presenter a la Mairie de
Ventabren,
Service de l' estat Civil, avant le 10 decembre 1990.

Stone or concrete vaults on sandy ground, covered with photographs and ceramic flowers. One with a stone dolphin. Cedric Kolesnitchenko 1979–1990. On the edge six small toy dolphins circle a larger blue one. Plaque with a bird on a branch saying "Fauvette, si tu voles autour de cette tombe, chante lui ta plus belle chanson". Another saying "Helloe Picacedrico". La Blanche.

Roman Port. Tour Sud. Stone neatly carved IEAN BONAVIER, TERESE BRUNO MDCCLIII. Two banana skins and an empty cheese box (Donjon). HISTOBUS passes, a painted galley along its side.

Bus to Barjols. Jean-Luc and Colette. Drinks in L' Europe.

THE VEIN

Cabinet of boxes for boules. "Momi" a small pastis. Ses 28 fontaines, 12 lavoires. Raclette with Riette and Yves. Two degrees. Ice inside the windows of the studio. White plumes on the head of St.Marcel. Spark from boule hitting a stone. Dropping pieces of the bridge onto the ice. Swinging down trees with Jean-Luc into the cave, leaves curled with frost underfoot.

a reliable testing ground

gardens inside shelters

shades patterning

an idealised culture

in one landscaped clump

stuffed full of shells

a version or remnant of something

under a different name

some crisis of identity

spanned the world

thought was the only thing

to come back to acting

beyond acoustics

even when dramatic

she always wore fancy dress

simply cut and held low

objects grouped together

confidently into fine jewellery

after the storm new scents

touched by salt spray

hardly dimmed the harsh light

he sometimes pulled at his hair

obsessed with finding the beautiful

curtain allowing him entry

never able to follow

the middle of night

downwards to find a runway

with deep sides

writhing under his fingers

personalities full of energy

order a series

of the same programme

cool for film

using this knowledge

machines talk to themselves

maintain a very persistent

buzzing as the signal

ends in a dramatic freeze

close to the border

on a street with a few orange trees

7.30 a.m. Around the Vieux port. Empty plastic trays and scales. Up to the park. Cargo ship heading into basin: tug (lights) sailing in reverse at the stern. Water changing from dark to light grey. Overcast. Bonne Année sign out: several of the fluorescent tubes for the blue cross broken. Le Lutin shut. Two joggers in blue overalls. Dogs being walked. Back to the port. *Chantal* coming in to berth next to *Edmund Dantes*. Small boat for sale 8,000f. Man in bright red leggings puts up two white trestles, light green tray hinged along centre. Hauls in his lines. First two empty (curled flat into rope baskets) except for eight tiny fish thrown immediately to the seagulls. MA 489644, red band, ties up broadside to the quay. Man in yellow oilskins takes darker green trestle table from forward hold and puts it up. Washes out tray with sponge from yellow plastic bucket. Unties bowline, pushes out with foot, steps on board, reverses, then heads into space next to the sandwich kiosk. Man in MA 30837, tied up to tyre on the side of Agence de Voyages float, extracts a starfish from his net. Walking round to kiosk, I see the boat with red trim is the *Mathilde*. Owner is describing, with both arms, what looks like an enormous wave, laughing, to man from kiosk adjusting balloons (cloth cap, green jogging trousers with VOGUE in black stencil type down the leg). Some trays being filled with fish taken from a small grey van. CHAPPY moto pulling a two-wheeled cart laden with herbs drives along the quay and is unloaded, driver putting lemons into small wicker baskets. Patch of sunlight, noise of buses, crowds passing on their way to work. Two legionnaires waiting at the stop. Old men in plastic jackets wearing dark glasses.

Along under the road to Pont D'Arenc. Walk past douane while looking away. Past *Porto Cargo* (Bestia), rust streaks from anchor at bow. Past parked containers, one open loaded with cork bark. Over the swing bridge painted red lead, ochre, grey-green with an occasional purple cross-truss. Through a narrow stone arch almost filled with a rusting pipe, tiny stalactites, and out onto the digue. Massive concrete squares, about two-yards all ways, dropped anyhow onto the seaward side. Small fishing boat, MA 663746, stern to digue, man paying out line, water spurting from starboard scupper as she rolls. The *El-Djazair* from Algiers, manoeuvering to dock, reverses into the basin, bow swinging out. Red and black pilot boat speeds up, catches pale green hawser, and pulls her around. Below me a man in a red shirt pisses against the side of an enormous rusted iron tank. Three siren blasts from the ferry hull-down on the horizon past the Chateau d'If. Sky, light, horizon, colour of sea, all constantly changing. As I reach the lighthouse a white Renault "Clan", with Service de Pilotage 24 painted on its side pulls up and a man goes into the office. A couple of fishermen at the very tip. A large metal '98'. half the 9 broken off, the rest pulled out from the stone, is what I'm level with, walking back, as the *Ti Pasa* (Alger) slowly passes me. An empty square padlocked metal cage on top of the digue.

At the top of the steps at the end of Rue des Belles Ecuelles two Arabs sit on a wooden bench in the sun. From inside the jacket of one pokes the head of a white parrot. A short fat man rolls a bright blue gas cylinder down the centre railings of Montée des Accoules.

MARSEILLE DECEMBER 1990–FEBRUARY 1991

A LETTER TO MARTIN STANNARD

Dear Martin,

I thought I'd pretty clearly stated my method in *El Barco del Abismo* over twenty years ago, and I don't think it's changed much. Perhaps it's more juggling than attaching now. So what I'll do is give you the context of the last poem I wrote a couple of days ago. Just before midnight I was walking home after dinner with Jean-Luc Sarré and his wife Christine, the worse for anisette and Buzet. I remember being, while pissing, fascinated by a bright yellow sign advertising a garage: so much so I had to approach it and rub the wall with my fingers to make sure the painted shadow wasn't real. I went on down hill into the city and some minutes later stopped at a stall for a sandwich (tournedos et frites: 13f). No-one about. The owner, Tunisian, listening to loud radio in Arabic. As he rolled the sandwich in paper, twisting the ends and adding a pink paper napkin, he switched the channel and we heard the news flash of the start of war. We shrugged at one another with eyes and mouth. And as I went round by the port. the water dark grey and calm

> sitting there watching
>
> air decay
>
> between the levels
>
> of white tiles

started running through my head. At the bottom of the 39 steep long steps leading up the Montée des Accoules I wrote them down in pencil on the back of a scrap of blue graph paper on the other side of which was

> Julien t'attend a 20h au New York
>
> Livraison cuisiniere demain matin avant 11h.

About eleven the next morning, after opening the shutters and watching the Arab girl opposite lean over the bright red shoes on the windowsill to shout down into the street I walked over to the Centre. Clear blue sky, sunlight hitting the roofs, a cold wind through the narrow stone passageways. The exhibition on at the moment is of Jean Cocteau's time in the South. Quite boring, lots of xeroxes of cards to his mother with Xs marking his room, endless photographs of Jean Cocteau with Luis Dominguin, Jean Cocteau with Eddie Constantine, Jean Cocteau with Gina Lollobrigida. I made a quick sketch of a chicken with yellow feet, labelled it *Coq Jaune-Toe* and gave it to Emmanuel who gave me in return a letter from Franco. The news that Patrizia Vicinelli had died a couple of days previously. I remembered the last time I'd seen her husband Gianni Castagnoli, exhausted at a bar table in Milan. And started listing images of Patrizia in my mind: dancing at 3am in the Lucky Bar only five years ago . . . a warm afternoon by the lake at Geneva with John Higgins . . . rushing all the way across town for a quick coffee with Val and Giovanni D'Agostino at the café near his Studio . . . forcing herself to speak, and even to scribble a rough alphabet, after the stroke. An image of falling flickered through, and on the back of Franco's envelope I scribbled

tangles of wire

toppling her to the ground

Back in my room; L-shaped, a table, a bed, a lamp, two chairs. I tried to work at some drawings for the walls. But couldn't concentrate. I walked down the various flights of steps to the port, turned right past the fifties (architect: Pouillon) blocks replacing the part of the Old Town completely destroyed by the Germans in 1943, thinking of a plan of Marseille printed in 1950 that Emmanuel had shown me, with just a white blank on the map for the whole area. I continued along, under the new concrete highway, beside the docks, to the main gate. Loitered until the two Customs Officers were occupied searching the bags of three black sailors leaving. Slid through the other side and past the rows of containers, rusting, some cracked open, one pallet stacked with cork bark, up a stone tunnel almost filled with an iron pipe and small stalactites and out onto the digue. There I spent the afternoon, alone, walking the length of it, watching the *Ti Pasa* come in from Algiers, the *Emerald Light* (rusty, heavy at the stern, listing to port) leave for Dublin, a couple of fishing boats rolling in the swell. Clouds flickered over, the sea and horizon changed colour continuously. When I got back to my room on the envelope was

> by the side of the numbers
>
> polished petrol tank
>
> unlike what he saw
>
> leaned down and picked up
>
> hoardings jutted out

Evening. Water running down the central groove of the stone steps as the cleaners, blue trousers obviously standard issue and size, as the white inverted 'v' on the leg, sometimes cut off, sometimes with six inches of colour below it, showed, swept away the day's dog-shit. The plastic bags of rubbish, handles tied into rabbit-ears, already

on each corner. I wrote some letters, closed the shutters,
switched on the lamp and listened to the news

> ejected from the real
>
> far away breathing
>
> to hold on to
>
> gloved fingers meshing
>
> > appeared.

Before going to sleep I played with the lines, taking four-
teen as the length I've been happy with for a while. In
the morning I read it again with the windows open, chill
wind through the room, coffee spitting on the hotplate:

> sitting there watching
>
> air decay
>
> between the levels
>
> of white tiles
>
> he saw
>
> tangles of wire
>
> a polished petrol tank
>
> hoardings jutted out
>
> by the side of numbers

to hold on to

far away breathing.

ejected from the real

gloved fingers meshing

toppling her to the ground

(in memoriam Patrizia Vicinelli)

regards,

Tom

Lightning Source UK Ltd.
Milton Keynes UK
UKHW021019220322
400428UK00005B/236